THEODOR VON HOLST
HIS ART AND THE PRE-RAPHAELITES

I amuse myself with playing the harp a little and when my fingers get sore I get out on the sea shore. There I sit and brood, giving full scope and swing to my Ideas:- no one to disturb me, nothing around but sky, sea and sand. Ah! Quel délice. Then, when the tide is low, I sketch a little on the sands to astonish the oysters, come home, whistle for an hour, read Hoffmann, then get dinner prepared and watch another hour at the window for Gustavus.

(Cat.2)

SELF-PORTRAIT WITH BROTHER, GUSTAVUS CIRCA 1832-37, CAT.3

MAX BROWNE

THEODOR VON HOLST
HIS ART AND THE PRE-RAPHAELITES

1810 - 2010

A BICENTENARY EXHIBITION AT
THE HOLST BIRTHPLACE MUSEUM
CHELTENHAM

FOR OSCAR, WHO I HOPE WILL
NOT BE AS ROMANTIC AS HIS FATHER

First published in Great Britain in 2010 by
The Holst Birthplace Museum
4 Clarence Road
Cheltenham GL52 2AY
Tel. 01242 524846
www.holstmuseum.org.uk

on the occasion of the Bicentenary Exhibition of paintings,
drawings, prints and letters of Theodor von Holst held in
the 200th year of his birth at the Holst Birthplace Museum,
Cheltenham 3 September - 11 December 2010.

ISBN 13 978-0-9563769-0-9

Very great thanks are due to our sponsors without whom this
project would not have been possible. The considerable costs
of printing the catalogue, of transporting works to and from
the exhibition in accordance with the government indemnity
insurance scheme and other such requirements have meant that
we have relied on their generosity. Likewise the support and
enthusiasm of the lenders of works to the exhibition has been
unanimous, unfailing and often exceptional.

The Trustees of The Holst Birthplace Museum gratefully
acknowledge the following individuals, businesses and
organisations for their essential financial contributions in
realising this Bicentenary Exhibition:-

BEECHWOOD SHOPPING CENTRE
CHELTENHAM ARTS COUNCIL
CHELTENHAM SURFACING LTD.
CHELTENHAM DFAS
WEST MERCIA DFAS
THE CHARLES IRVING CHARITABLE TRUST
THE HOLST FOUNDATION
KINGSCOTT DIX (CHELTENHAM) LTD.
NINA ZBOROWSKA
POTTER & HOLMES ARCHITECTS

Cheltenham Decorative and Fine Arts Society

Designed by Max Browne
Made and printed by Action Colour
Units 9C/D/E
Alstone Lane Trading Estate, Cheltenham, Gloucestershire
GL51 8HF
Tel. 01242 584312
www.actioncolour.com

CONTENTS

FRONT COVER
THE BRIDE (BRITISH INSTITUTION 1842) CAT.42

BACK COVER
THE WISH (BRITISH INSTITUTION 1841) CAT.41

FOREWORD

My interest in Theodor von Holst reaches back to the heady 1960s when paintings flooded through the London salerooms at the rate of at least five hundred a week, and minor masterpieces could be bought by a shrewd eye for a very few pounds and half an ounce of knowledge. In the gloom of Bonham's it was the escutcheon on the ruined frame that I first noticed, loose and lopsided, bearing the legend "The Fortune Teller. Von Holst. From the Collection of Lord Northwick 1859." As for twelve months or so in 1964-65 I had played some part in the final dispersal of the Northwick Collections and knew of this painting from a detailed record of Lord Northwick's Picture Gallery painted in the mid 1840s, my determination to buy this so-called Fortune Teller was a powerful but entirely sentimental response. She has since been my companion for far longer than most marriages.

But who, in the mid-Sixties, was von Holst? For Lord Northwick, many of whose paintings went to the National Gallery on his death, to have brought this picture straight from the easel, so to speak, he must have had some reputation. In my pre-war Thieme-Becker, the Septuagint for art historians, he accounted for five column inches of bare facts, in my post-war Bénézit, only one - and it is worth noting that from all dictionaries of art since published, he has been omitted. As Thieme-Becker told me that von Holst had, as a boy, been the pupil of Henry Fuseli at the Royal Academy, I showed my Fortune Teller to Gert Schiff, the indefatigable hunter of all things Fuselian and probably then the only art historian in the world who knew of von Holst. It was he who later told Max Browne of it, and Max who published it in 1994 together with every other painting then known to be by von Holst when he presented this forgotten genius to an indifferent world one hundred and fifty years after his death.

With an exhibition and catalogue Max put an end to that indifference. There cannot be an art historian, an art dealer, an art expert at Christie's, Sotheby's or Bonham's still in ignorance of Theodor von Holst. Max Browne's first catalogue put him on everybody's bookshelves and provided an authoritative work of reference very much in the scholarly mould of his mentor, Gert Schiff; not only did it provide all the conventional apparatus of an academic catalogue, a checklist of paintings lost and found, a summary of Christie's sale of the contents of his studio on his death in 1844 and an appendix on drawings that made clear how misleadingly close he came to Fuseli, it demonstrated how European an artist von Holst was, how aware of German Romantic art and how reliant on German literature for his narratives.

Most art historians would have considered done in 1994 the Herculean labour of disinterring von Holst, of clarifying the confusion of his drawings with those of Fuseli, of giving him a recogniseable identity and arousing an international interest that has brought about the inclusion of his work in such major exhibitions as *Gothic Nightmares* at Tate Britain in 2006 and *Bohèmes* in Paris, Madrid and Budapest in 2012. But Max has not let go of Theodor; driven by passionate enthusiasm and connoisseurship that match his scrupulous scholarship, his new catalogue is far more than a corrected edition of the old and incorporates all that he has discovered in the intervening years - new paintings, new sources, new documents, new facts, making von Holst an even more substantial painter. I do not suppose that he will ever let go of this precocious genius, this pornographer for the Prince Regent, this associate of a notorious poisoner, this husband of a jealous wife prepared to end his philandering with her stiletto.

Brian Sewell

PREFACE AND ACKNOWLEDGEMENTS

The Holst Birthplace Museum is primarily devoted to the composer Gustav Holst (1874-1934). However it is extremely proud of its association with Theodor von Holst, and continues to collect both work and archive material relating to him. Theodor is an integral part of the Holst story, enhancing our understanding of Gustav Holst, in terms of his heritage and artistic background. The creative talents of the von Holsts were many and varied, going back to Gustav Holst's great-grandfather Matthias (1767-1845), the father of Gustavus and Theodor. The fact that Gustav Holst was so musically talented is not surprising when seen in the context of his forbears.

Amongst the items donated to the then Cheltenham Art Gallery and Museums* in 1974 by Gustav Holst's daughter Imogen Holst, is Theodor von Holst's double portrait of himself and his brother, Gustavus (1799-1870). Gustavus was Gustav Holst's grandfather, also a musician, and the first of the family to settle in Cheltenham. The painting now hangs in the splendour of the Holst Birthplace Museum's Regency Room. In 1996 a particularly striking painting by Theodor was added to the collection of his work at Cheltenham Art Gallery & Museums. This was the erotically charged *Bertalda Frightened by Apparitions*, firmly part of his romantic output. It fits well with the deep red interior of the Regency Room, flanked by furniture and decorative art of the period.

The organisation of *Theodor von Holst his Art and the Pre-Raphaelites* has been prompted by the bicentenary of Theodor von Holst's birth. However it comes at a time when there appears to be a growing recognition of his art. New discoveries have been made, such as the *Portrait of Jessy Harcourt* and *Caesarini and the Soldier in the Forest* exhibited for the first time in the public sphere in this current exhibition.

As an independent Museum with a small staff, curating an exhibition like this involves an enormous amount of work. I would like to thank all the Volunteers and Trustees who have helped to make the exhibition possible, in particular Jenny Ogle for fundraising; Liz Auster, for events; and Sara Salvidge, Education Assistant, for creating an education programme. I would also like to thank Christopher Fletcher for research advice, Steven Blake for proofreading, and Helen Brown from Cheltenham Art Gallery & Museum for her help with the Holst collection and archive.

Lastly I would like to thank Max Browne, who I have worked with closely over the last eighteen months in curating the show, and who has written the central essay on Theodor von Holst.

Laura Kinnear
Curator, Holst Birthplace Museum

* The Holst Birthplace Museum became an independent trust in 2000.

Somewhere out there, unknown to us, hundreds of drawings and exquisite watercolours by Theodor von Holst are waiting to be re-discovered. Along with dozens of his lost, often unsigned, dramatic paintings this seemingly sad state of affairs actually means we have much to look forward to. After more than thirty years the thrill of seeing a 'new Holst' still feels, to me, like welcoming a lost relative back into the fold.

As a schoolboy my favourite classical piece was *The Planets*, our school boathouse was opposite the Holst family house at Barnes Bridge and my father had been to St. Paul's. As an unashamed romantic and frustrated non-artist it was only a matter of time, in exploring Romantic art, before I discovered my mission. In 1976 I saw an illustration of an etching by Theodor in a book and was hooked. The same year I contacted the great Fuseli scholar Gert Schiff, met the art dealer Brian Sewell (and his 'Fortune Teller') and Imogen Holst took me to visit the museum she had recently set up in Cheltenham to honour her father. We had a picnic lunch on a park bench and then she showed me the family pictures and memorabilia.

In 1972 the Tate bought their first Holst painting - they have remained champions of his art ever since. In 2006 curator Martin Myrone placed Theodor's darker side in the mainstream of British Romantic Art by featuring him alongside Fuseli, Blake and Gillray in the groundbreaking *Gothic Nightmares* exhbition. In 2012 Alison Smith will also present Holst, as a precursor to the art of Rossetti, Millais and their circle, in the most extensive Pre-Raphaelite exhibition ever staged. I am grateful to both for their encouragement and enthusiasm.

With this snowballing momentum I approached the Holst Birthplace Museum to enquire if there would be interest in some sort of bicentenary celebration for Gustav's great-uncle. The response was immediate and positive and has grown into what you see before you. To paraphrase B.R. Haydon - I am so pleased and Theodor will be too!

The welcome I received from Laura Kinnear and the Trustees of the museum was inspiring and I hope the result eighteen months later is the same for them. It has been a pleasure working with Laura and the Trustees intimately responsible for various aspects of this project. I would particularly like to congratulate Jenny Ogle for achieving wonders in raising the funds necessary to realise the Bicentenary Celebration. For help with the catalogue I would like to express my gratitude to Lindsay Stainton, David Weinglass, Franny Moyle, Martin Myrone and Alison Smith. Acknowledgement to the generous lenders, sponsors and others will be found in its pages.

Brian Sewell has, as ever, provided a bedrock of support and made me blush again.

Max Browne

THE FAMILY BACKGROUND OF THEODOR VON HOLST

Imogen Holst was very much aware of her family's artistic and musical background. Although on Gustav Holst's mother's side – the Lediard and Whately families - there was musical talent, their local Gloucestershire roots did not capture Imogen Holst's imagination as much as the von Holsts.[1] The von Holsts, descended from Central and Eastern Europe and Russia, enchanted Imogen, and she writes animatedly in her biography of her father about her great-great grandfather Matthias, who left his home city of Riga, Latvia for St Petersburg, Russia, to teach harp to the Imperial Russian Court.[2] Matthias later moved to England with his Russian wife Katherina, their eldest son Gustavus, and their elder two daughters, Caroline and Benigna.[3]

The Origins of the Holst family

In the biographies of Gustav Holst, his 'Swedish' ancestry is frequently alluded to. For example, in an early short biographical sketch from 1926, Richard Cappell writes: 'He was of Swedish extraction on his father's side; English on his mother's.'[4] Michael Short in his comprehensive biography of the composer also refers to his ancestry as 'Scandinavian.'[5] However this lineage is disputed, most notably by Harro H. Lange, a distant relative of Gustav Holst, who has researched the origins of the family, tracing them as far back as 16th century Germany.[6] According to Lange, the first registered name is Stephan Holste[7] (c1550-1610), a pastor, based in Basedow near Malchin, in the Duchy of Mecklenburg. The Holste family appear to have remained in Mecklenburg until the late 17th century. However, despite the Swedish ancestry being argued against, it should be remembered that Sweden was at the height of its territorial powers during the 16th and 17th centuries, holding much of Germany, including Mecklenburg. Significantly one of the individuals responsible for making Sweden one of the great powers of Europe was King Gustav Adolphus. His name was an obvious influence on the von Holst family for their offspring, and is perhaps suggestive of some acknowledgment of Swedish ancestry or affinity with the Swedish Empire.

The link with Mecklenburg effectively ended when a Lorenz Christian Holst (1673-?) left Rostock, the largest city in Mecklenburg, and emigrated to Riga, Latvia in 1703.[8] During this period Riga was also part of the Swedish Empire. Lorenz became a merchant in the city, later becoming Doyen of the Great Guild.[9] He married Anna Hollander, whose father was Matthias Hollander, also a merchant. Lorenz and Anna had at least fifteen children, including Meno Holst (b?-1805). Meno Holst, like his father and grandfather, was also a merchant. He married Marie Saumann, resulting in a son, Matthias

Holst (1769-1845), who clearly broke with family tradition by becoming a musician. He was the father of Gustavus and Theodor, and the founder of the English branch of Holsts.

The prefix 'von', denoting nobility, seems only to have been adopted once the Holsts emigrated, and even then, not until the mid 1820s. Interestingly it is the Holst offspring who appear to have been the first to adopt it. Matthias does not use the 'von' in any of his published scores, in contrast to Gustavus who uses it for all of his. Matthias does sign his name 'Matthias von Holst', although not until the late 1820s – probably once his children had embraced it. Presumably, calling yourself 'von Holst' was felt to be advantageous in the uncertain world of music and art.[10] Interestingly when Gustav Holst was required to drop the 'von' in his name during WW1, due to its Germanic connotations, he discovered his family had never actually been entitled to use it.

Matthias Holst 1769-1845

Matthias' family background seems to have been fairly prosperous: his father Meno was the head of a merchants' guild[11], and his grandparents were also involved with the city's commerce. It is not recorded how Matthias decided upon music as a career, although by the end of the 18th century he was living in St Petersburg, Russia, employed as a pianist, composer and harp teacher to the Imperial Russian Court. [12] It was at the Russian Court that he met Katherina Rogge, who became his wife.[13] It is thought that Katherina was part of the Imperial Russian family, and indeed a miniature of a Prince Rogge (fig.2), Katherina's brother, has survived, and is part of the collection on permanent display at the Holst Birthplace Museum.

Fig.2 *Prince Rogge* miniature

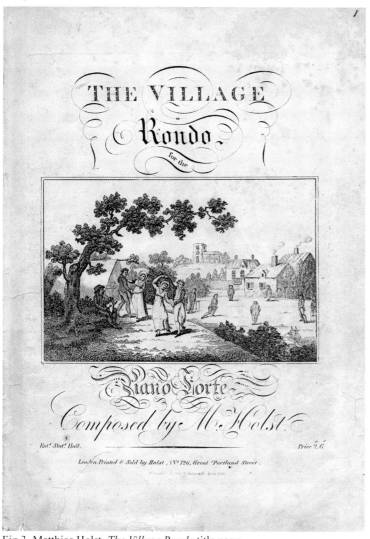

Fig.3 Matthias Holst, *The Village Rondo* title page

All of the secondary sources ascribe the Holsts' flight from Russia to political reasons.[14] The precise date of their departure is unknown, although it is likely to be 1804 at the latest, due to the existence of a christening record in London for their youngest daughter Constantia. The date of her birth is documented 11th November 1804, and her christening 28th April 1805. Imogen Holst in her biography of her father writes:

> He [Matthias] *came by boat to England. It was an unknown country to him. He had no friends there, and no prospects of getting any work, and at first he found it difficult to understand the language. But it seemed an hospitable place for an exile, and he unpacked his harps and his music in a house near Fitzroy Square and began searching London for piano pupils.[15]*

However, it is also possible that Matthias and Katherina left Russia for personal reasons – perhaps their relationship wasn't approved of. Even though Matthias was an educated and cultured man, he was from the mercantile classes, not the aristocracy like Katherina. An interesting source to perhaps support this idea is the marriage record for Matthias and Katherina in 1808, which is documented as taking place in Westminster, London. Thus Matthias and Katherina were not

married when they came to England, and indeed had four illegitimate children. However it is equally possible that they married again to formalise matters in their adopted country. Musically we know that Matthias was active in England from at least 1807 – in that year he was responsible for the incidental music for the play *Ulthona the Sorceress* at the Sans Pareil Theatre in the Strand[16].

It is not known if he wrote any further music specifically for the theatre, although he continued to compose and arrange, and had over fifty of his compositions and arrangements published over a thirty year period.[17] His pieces include: *The Village Rondo[18]* (fig.3)*; The Cottage Rondo; The Italian Momfrina;* and *A Selection of Scottish Melodies Arranged for the Voice with Symphonies and Accompaniments For the Spanish Guitar.* [19]

The von Holsts lived for most of their lives in Howland Street[20] and did not move away from the fashionable middle-class Fitzroy Square area until Katherina died in 1838. Their five children also seemed to have lived in the area, known as Fitzrovia, once they moved out of the family home. When Katherina died she was buried in the new All Souls Cemetery in Kensal Green[21], at the age of 68. At the time of her death she is listed as living at 44 Upper Charlotte Street, St. Pancras - around the corner from Howland Street where she and Matthias and their young family first came to live.

Only six years later Theodor joined his mother at All Souls – he is listed as living at the time of his death at 2 Percy Street, St. Pancras, again very close to Fitzrovia.[22] When Matthias died in 1845, a year after his son, at the impressive age of 86, he had moved to 37 Mary Street, Hampstead Road, St Pancras. Like Katherina and Theodor, he too was buried at All Souls.

Gustavus von Holst 1799-1870 -The First 'Cheltenham' Holst

Gustavus was the eldest of the Holst children, and the first of the Cheltenham Holsts. He appears to have been very close to his younger brother Theodor, who was born when Gustavus was ten. From the surviving correspondence Gustavus comes across as a cultured, witty and often sarcastic man; quick to criticise his patrons for their demands and affectations. He also seems to have had strong family ties, for example in one of his letters to his parents when they were away in Riga in 1827 he writes:

> We are all overjoyed that you have decided to return to us: One is more thought of en famille than alone, I think we would gain more if we were together than being now alone and [?], independent of the happiness of being together. I shall expect your next letter with impatience to know whether you have taken any steps to your leaving Riga...[23]

It appears that one of the reasons for Matthias and Katherina travelling to Riga was to organise a retrospective birth certificate for Gustavus. This certificate, drawn up in Riga in 1827 survives, as does a note recording his birth in 1799. The retrospective document contains the name of two of Kathcrina's Rogge relations as witnesses. [24]

In the 1827 letter Gustavus shows concern for his parents' financial circumstances, 'I am surprised to learn that a Ruble [sic] is only tenpence, I fancied it was 3/6 which makes me think you must be in want of money.' By this period, at the age of twenty-eight, Gustavus, like his father, was a musician and teacher. He writes with evident disappointment: 'My pupils have not increased since my last letter…' He also offers a glimpse into the life of a musician at the time: 'I played at Madam De Vigo's Concert which was given at Sir F: Burdetts the 16 May and that the De La Torre's give their Grand Banquet Feast the 4 of May', and hints at some of the difficulties: 'I think you know already that I have broken with Sedlelatzek, he is a selfish dog.' A joint letter[25] (fig.4) written by Theodor and Gustavus to their parents five years later is equally waspish about another of Gustavus' patrons, the Burlingtons of Eastbourne. This letter, dated Saturday and Sunday October 13th/14th 1832, is significant as it reveals Gustavus' peripatetic lifestyle as a musician and teacher, as well as the relationship between the brothers. Theodor has gone to stay with his brother, and interestingly reveals himself also to be musical: 'I amuse myself with playing the harp a little and when my fingers get sore I get out on the sea shore.'

The letter is written from Eastbourne, then an up-and-coming seaside resort, and therefore an ideal place for a musician and teacher to find work amongst fashionable society. However things did not seem to be going particularly well. Theodor writes that Gustavus is worn out and bored by the demands of the aristocratic Burlingtons: 'Gustavus has been at Lady C's each day from 12 till 5 o'clock and in the Evening from 8 till 11… In fact he has serious thoughts of cutting it altogether.' Gustavus himself adds:

> The weather is become very much better, yet I am heartily sick of it. The Burlington Family engross the whole of my time and begrudge every hour that I am not with them. If there were a magician or even a fortune teller here I should be tempted to enquire if any return will be made for this great sacrifice of time and labour.

Clearly this is not the life Gustavus dreamt of leading, and to vent some of his frustration, he and Theodor decided to go on a twenty-two mile walk from Eastbourne to Brighton. The cold, wet October did not extinguish the brother's romantic spirits. Theodor writes:

> We had but trudged some way up the Hills when we found ourselves gradually incircled [sic] by Mist first whirling in Eddies on the heights above then rolling in magnetic and mysterious grandeur like Nature's Pall we were wet to the

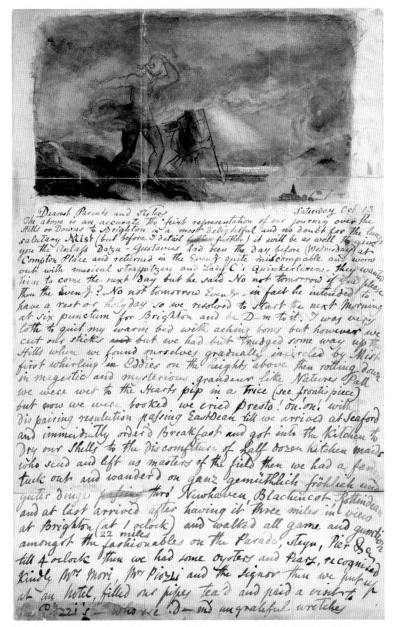

Fig.4 Family letter from Theodor and Gustavus von Holst, 1832 (cat.2)

> Hearts pip in a trice (see frontispiece) but now we were booked we cried presto! On! On!

Theodor accompanied this imaginative prose with a hazy watercolour sketch of the brothers struggling in the inclement conditions. Once the ramblers reached Brighton, fortified by their exertions and 'oysters and pears', they 'walked all game and gumption amongst the fashionables', some of whom Theodor calls,'d-md ungrateful wretches.'

It is not known how long Gustavus remained in Eastbourne, although we know that he was in Southampton around this period too: the 1832 letter mentions a 'Miss Moffatt' from the city, whom Gustavus is trying to order some sheet music for. It is likely that Gustavus followed where fashionable society led: to the places where young ladies required music masters. It is therefore not a surprise that Gustavus' path eventually led to Cheltenham – then an important town for employment during the season when the fashionable people were in town.

However Gustavus also had other things going on in his life apart from composing, teaching and flattering aristocrats. His personal life in the early 1830s was changing. Around this period Gustavus met Honoria Goodrich, who in 1841 was to become his wife. Honoria, whose first name is often shortened to Honor, and whose surname is written as both Goodrich and Goodrick, gave birth to the first of their two illegitimate children, Gustavus Matthias, who became known as Matthias, 14th November 1833. In the 1841 census Gustavus is listed as a Professor of Music, and living in Fitzroy Place with Honoria and his two children, Matthias 7 and their second child Katherine 1. Honoria is recorded as a 'Holst.' The census was undertaken in June; their marriage did not take place until 4th December 1841, where Honoria is listed as residing at a separate address in Kentish Town. Both the spouses' fathers were witnesses at their marriage: Matthias and Isaac Goodrich. Isaac's occupation is not written clearly on the marriage certificate, although it looks like 'Farmer.' Honoria came from Wellingham, a small village in Norfolk, and it is likely that her social background was quite different to that of Gustavus. A will survives of an Isaac Goodrick from Wellingham, presumably Honoria's father, which was drawn up in 1822.[26] In the will Isaac's occupation is a carpenter and although he does own some type of property the total value of his effects was a relatively low £20.

After Gustavus and Honoria married they had three more children: Lorenz in 1843, Adolphus – the father of Gustav Holst – in 1846, and Benigna in 1848. All of the children were born in London.

Because of his work Gustavus spent long periods away from home and Honoria. His earliest recorded visit to Cheltenham is in 1833, where he announces in both the *Cheltenham Chronicle* and the *Cheltenham Journal* that he intends to make a stay in the town for the autumn. [27] This stay may have prevented him from being in London for the birth of his son in November.

The von Holst sisters: Benigna, Caroline and Constantia

Matthias and Katherina also had three daughters: Benigna (1801-45); Caroline (1802-?) and Constantia (1804-?). Of these sisters we know the most about Constantia. This is because of the surviving letter[28] she wrote to her parents in 1827 with her brothers Gustavus and Theodor. We also know what Constantia looked like: two portraits by Theodor of her survive, and she was also a model for him in a number of other works.

The 1827 letter contains a watercolour portrait of her by Theodor (fig.5). The portrait shows Constantia at 22 and in her own words is offered: '…not from any vanity – no – only that you may not entirely forget your affectionate Constantia.' There is a warmth and affection in Constantia's letter; she writes how happy she is

Fig.5 Portrait of Constantia von Holst, by Theodor, on a family letter, 1827

at, '…receiving hope of seeing you soon', and she races between sending love to her parents and sisters and wistfully dreaming of the career she may embark upon:

> I pass my time as well as I can, in practising singing, for I will tell you candidly my hope and intentions if they are frivolous, and not according to your wishes then tell me that I may give them up whatever you think pray in your next don't forget to mention…I think I improve in singing and by the time you come back to sing much better, then if I was apprenticed to a singing master, for a year – and come out as an actress or singer that I might gain money – what pleasure it would be!

It seems that Constantia shared her family's interest in the arts and possessed musical talent. It is also clear that she was concerned about her financial position in the future, and this together with Gustavus' comments about saving money to send to his parents', and the problems with his own career suggest that the von Holst financial position was somewhat precarious.

There are no indications that Constantia embarked upon singing or acting; what is known is that in 1833 she married a Frenchman, Jean Furcy Tourrier, a Professor of Languages, and had four children, one of whom, Juliette died at the age of ten. Constantia's love for her brothers is indicated by the names of two of her children: Theodore, born 2 years after her brother died, and Gustavus.

Benigna and Caroline were also artistic. Indeed Benigna created a large body of drawings and paintings, although only one of her sketches survives.[29] She married Charles Weiss in 1828, with whom she moved to India, dying there with him in 1845. When Caroline married Joachim Heinrich Christian Fredericks in 1834 many family members were present: Matthias, Constantia, and Theodor. Caroline was musical, and according to Imogen Holst became a harpist in the Prussian Court.[30]

Gustavus von Holst and Cheltenham

When Gustavus advertised in the *Cheltenham Chronicle* and the *Cheltenham Journal* in 1833 he described himself as '…the celebrated Harpist', and offering 'harp lessons in the town and neighbourhood.' In the 18th and 19th centuries the harp was considered a suitable instrument for females to play, and many were purchased for the domestic sphere. Gustavus would have taught women to play in their own homes and they would probably have played some of his own compositions and arrangements; by the 1830s he had published several works, such as: *Buono Notte! Serenade for the harp* (fig.6); *Love's Complaint and the Swiss Song of Home arranged for the harp*; *The Harpist's Sketchbook*, and Beethoven's *Grand Septett*, dedicated to Miss Moffatt.[31]

Theodor came to visit Gustavus in Cheltenham during his stay in 1833. We know this because of the existence of a watercolour sketch, *Hero and Leander* (fig.7), which is inscribed 'Cheltenham 1833.'

It seems that Cheltenham proved profitable for Gustavus – he continued to make yearly visits to the spa town from London, placing regular advertisements in the local press. Initially he stayed in rented accommodation in North Place, although he is known at various addresses in the town, including: the High Street, Tivoli Place, Clarence Parade, Queen's Circus, and Rotunda Terrace, where he eventually settled.

From the mid 1850s Gustavus was a permanent resident of the town. By this stage both his parents, his sister Benigna and of course his brother Theodor had died. His remaining sisters were married with families. His wife Honoria had also bore him three more children. Gustavus did not have the family ties he once had in the city – perhaps it made more sense to him now to move his family to Cheltenham for good. The family left London at some point after 1851 – in the census of that year the whole family, apart from Gustavus is listed as living at 73 Upper Norton Street London. It is likely that Gustavus was away teaching, probably in Cheltenham. However by the time of the 1861 census they were living in Cheltenham, at 16 Rotunda Terrace. Gustavus is listed as 'Professor of Music, Harp and Piano Forte.' His birthplace is listed as: 'Russia, Naturalised British Subject',

Fig.6 Gustavus von Holst, *Buenna Notte! Serenade for the Harp* titlepage

reflecting the fact that he had become a British Citizen in 1846.[32] By this stage his eldest son, Matthias had left home, leaving Kate, 21; Lorenz, 18; Adolphus, 15; and Benigna, 12.

Cheltenham in the 1850s and 1860s was a much more sedate place than it had been in its halcyon spa days of the early 1800s. Even when Gustavus first started to come to the town in the 1830s, the spa's attractions like the taste for Regency excesses were beginning to wane. According to Arthur Bell, '…gaiety and pleasure in its purest form lasted only about 30 or 40 years.'[33] The party was effectively over by the 1840s, and a different mood and attitude prevailed; one which favoured church and education over balls and assemblies, ushered in by the Reverend Francis Close. Respectable society was just what Gustavus needed of course: nice middle and upper-class families with daughters requiring suitable diversion.

Nevertheless it seems that the Cheltenham families were not quite lucrative enough; Gustavus continues to be listed in directories in London whilst also living in Cheltenham. For example in 1848 he is listed as Professor of the Harp at 73 Upper Norton Street; in 1860 he is listed as a Professor of Music at 22 Nottingham Place Marylebone.[34]

Adolphus von Holst

Gustavus' son Adolphus (1846-1901), the father of Gustav Holst also became a musician and teacher. Father and son seem to have worked together in much the same way as Adolph and Gustav did in the 1880s. Sadly Gustav Holst was not to meet his grandfather, who died in 1870, four years before he was born. In his will Gustavus left everything to his 'beloved wife' Honoria, which according to the solicitor was 'under £5,000.'[35] After Gustavus died, Honoria moved to Scotland, living with her other son, Matthias, also a musician. In the 1871 census Adolph is lodging at 5 Clarence Parade, and is listed as a music teacher, although he was also a noted performer in the town. He was also organist of both St Paul's, and later All Saints. His teaching led him to meet Clara Lediard, a piano pupil, originally from Cirencester, who had moved to Cheltenham with her mother and sisters. The Lediard family owned 4 Pittville Terrace, now 4 Clarence Road. When Adolph and Clara married in 1871 they moved into 4 Pittville Terrace. Three years later they had the first of their two children: Gustavus Theodore von Holst – later shortened to the more familiar Gustav Holst.

Notes

1. For a history of Gustav Holst's Gloucestershire roots see Kinnear, L. and Fletcher, C. *The Lediards and Whatleys of Gloucestershire,* 2009
2. Holst, I., *Gustav Holst A Biography,* 1938, p.1
3. Imogen Holst writes that they came to England with 'their small son Gustavus'. It is thought that their two daughters, Caroline and Benigna had also been born at this stage, possibly in Danzig (now Gdansk), Poland.
4. Cappell, R., *The Musical Times* (1927) via www.jstor.org/pss912599.
5. Short, M., *Gustav Holst A Biography,* 1980, p.9.
6. I am grateful to Harro H. Lange, a Holst descendant, for his information about the family.
7. According to Lange, Holste had been shortened to Holst by the early 17th century.
8. Short, M., ibid.
9. This information has been provided by Lange.
10. According to Lange, Meno Holst's brother, Matthias (1721-1762), married Ursula Elisabeth von Skodeisky, resulting in two sons who acquired the 'von': Johann Valentin von Holst and Heinrich Christian von Holst. It was therefore Matthias's cousins and their descendants, not him and his descendants who were legally entitled to use it.
11. According to Lange, Meno was the Doyen of the Black Heads Guild (Schwarzen Haeupter).
12. Short, M., ibid.
13. After Katherina and Matthias emigrated, Katherina is usually anglicised to Catherine.
14. See Short, M., ibid. and Holst, I., ibid.
15. Holst, I., ibid.
16. Short, M., ibid. The theatre became *The Adelphi* in 1819.
17. Copies of his and Gustavus' music are in the Holst archive at Cheltenham Art Gallery & Museum.
18. According to Phillip Scowcroft in his article *Cricket and Music*, Holst's *Village Rondo is* the earliest known sheet music to depict the game on its cover. (www.musicweb-international.com/classrev/2001/jan01/sport_and_music.htm)

19. A facsimile edition of *A Selection of Scottish Melodies* was published in 1985 by Tecla, with a preface by Brian Jeffrey. Jeffrey writes, 'It is his only known contribution to the guitar, but the simple and well thought out accompaniments seem to suit these Scottish songs, with a welcome, unusual, attractive, and authentic additions to their repertore.' (www.tecla.com/catalog/0046.htm)
20. Unfortunately most of Howland Street, which joined Tottenham Court Road, was destroyed by air-raids during WWII. It was originally built between 1776 and 1801, and was therefore relatively new when the von Holsts moved in. (www.british-history.ac.uk/report.aspx?compid=65153.)
21. All Souls Cemetery was established in 1833. (www.kensalgreen.co.uk/)
22. This house is still standing.(www.british-history.ac.uk/report.aspx?compid=65153)
23. Gustav Holst archive, Cheltenham Art Gallery & Museum
24. Both of these documents are in the Gustav Holst archive, as above.
25. Gustav Holst archive, as above.
26. Norfolk Record Office Will of Isaac Goodrick: ANW, will register, 1823-1825, (1823) fo.43, no.37.
27. This information has been passed on to the Holst Birthplace Museum by Mike Grindley.
28. Gustav Holst archive, Cheltenham Art Gallery & Museum.
29. The author is grateful to Benigna's descendant, Glenys Walker, Melbourne, Australia, for this information.
30. Holst, I., op.cit. p.5.
31. There are copies in the Gustav Holst archive, Cheltenham Art Gallery & Museum.
32. Gustavus' naturalisation papers are held at the National Archives. The certificate was issued 7 July 1846.
33. Bell, A., *Pleasure Town Cheltenham 1830-1860*, Chalfont-St-Giles, 1981.
34. Holst, I., op.cit. p.4.
35. A copy is in the Gustav Holst archive, Cheltenham Art Gallery & Museum.

Bibliography

Bell, A., *Pleasure Town Cheltenham 1830-1860*, Richard Sadler, Chalfont St Giles 1981

Browne, M., *The Romantic Art of Theodor von Holst 1810-44*, Lund Humphries, London 1994

Holmes, P., *The Illustrated Lives of the Great Composers,* Holst Omnibus Press, London 1997

Holst, I., *Gustav Holst A Biography,* Oxford University Press, Oxford 1938 (new edition 1969)

Holst, I., *The Great Composers Holst,* Faber and Faber, London 1974 (new edition 1981)

Holst, I., *A Scrap-book for the Holst Birthplace Museum,* Hugh Tempest Radford, East Bergholt 1978

Kinnear, L. and Fletcher, C., *The Lediards and Whatleys of Gloucestershire: A Holst Family History,* Holst Birthplace Museum, Cheltenham 2009

Short, M., Gustav *Holst A Biography,* Oxford University Press, Oxford 1980

Internet sources

JSTOR: The Musical Times www.jstor.org/pss/912599
Music Web International www.musicweb-international.com/classrev/2001/jan01/sport_and_music.htm
Tecla www.tecla.com/catalog/0046.htm
All Souls Cemetery www.kensalgreen.co.uk
St Pancras www.british-history.ac.uk/report.aspx?compid=65153
Family history www.ancestry.co.uk
Adelphi Theatre www.adelphitheatre.co.uk/theatre-history.htm

Archival sources

Cheltenham Art Gallery & Museum, Gustav Holst Archive, Letters and birth certificates.
Norfolk Record Office, Will of Isaac Goodrick: ANW, will register, 1823-1825, (1823) fo.43, no.37.

Fig.7 *Hero and Leander* (inscribed 'Cheltenham 1833'), watercolour 25x19 cm, USA collection

Theodor von Holst, his art and the Pre-Raphaelites

Introduction

Let us go to a dark, fire-lit drawing-room in Mid-Victorian London where a thirty-four year old romantic artist and poet is writing his contribution to an historic forthcoming book:

" . . . Another painter, ranking far below David Scott, but still not to be forgotten where British poetic art is the theme – was Theodore von Holst, an Englishman, though of German extraction; in many of whose most characteristic works the influence of Blake, as well as Fuseli, has probably been felt. But Holst was far from possessing anything like the depth of thought or high aims which distinguished Blake. At the same time, his native sense of beauty and colour in the more ideal walks of art was originally beyond any of his contemporaries, except Etty and Scott. He may be best described, perhaps, to the many who do not know his works, as the Edgar Poe of painting; but lacking, probably, even the continuity of closely studied work in the midst of irregularities which distinguished the weird American poet, and has enabled him to leave behind some thing which cannot soon be forgotten. Holst, on the contrary, it is to be feared, has hardly transmitted such complete record of his naturally great gifts as can secure their rescue from oblivion. It would be very desirable that an account of him and his works should be written by someone best able to do so among those still living who must have known him. It is a tribute due to an artist who, however imperfect his self-expression during a short and fitful career, forms certainly one of the few connecting links between the early and sound period of English colour and method in painting, and that revival of which so many signs have in late years been apparent. At present, much of what he did is doubtless in danger of being lost altogether. Specimens from his hand existed in the late Northwick collection, now dispersed; and some years since I saw a most beautiful work by him – a female head or half-figure – among the pictures at Stafford House. But Holst's sketches and designs on paper (a legion past numbering) were for the most part more expressive of his full powers than his pictures, which were too often merely sketches enlarged without reference to nature. Of these, a very extensive collection was possessed by the late Sergeant Ralph Thomas. What has become of them? Among Holst's pictures, the best are nearly always those partaking of the fantastic or supernatural, which, however dubious a ground to take in art, was the true bent of his genius. A notable instance of his comparative weakness in subjects of pure dignity, may be found in what has been pronounced as his best work, and was probably the most 'successful' at the time of its production; that is, the *Raising of Jairus's Daughter*, which was lately in the the gallery at the Pantheon in Oxford Street, and probably still remains there."[1]

So ended Dante Gabriel Rossetti's tribute to his romantic predecessor, kindred spirit and painter hero published in 1863 (in Gilchrist's *The Life of William Blake, "Pictor Ignotus"*). Rossetti was only fifteen years old when Holst died suddenly from liver failure (and 'disappointment' according to B.R.Haydon and Lord Lytton) on Valentine's Day 1844, when only thirty-three. Although living close by in London both artists never met and it is regrettable that Holst never knew of his burgeoning young fan club. It is tantalising today to realise that we still know only a fraction of the fine paintings and drawings (fig.7) by Holst that Rossetti had been familiar with and which had so fired his admiration and his testimonial on Holst written in his *Supplementary* chapter for 'Blake's Life'.

My 1994 essay began with a vivid description of Holst's studio, by a visitor in 1827, which was published twenty years later in *The People's Journal*. It introduced the striking themes of his early productions amidst a plethora of medieval paraphernalia and his own kirtled presence – a theatrical step back into the popular medieval mode that was appreciated but never attempted by the Pre-Raphaelites themselves. Rossetti must have read this tribute to Holst since he cut out the accompanying engraving and mounted it on his wall, " . . as the sole pictorial adornment of my room" as he later described in his famous first letter to Ford Madox Brown.

Someone who did know Holst, however, was David Scott's brother and Rossetti's long-standing friend and confidant, William Bell Scott, another admirer of Blake and Holst. Born into a diligent, artistic and literary family in Edinburgh, his talent bought him to London in 1837 where he joined the circle of other young hopefuls seeking fame and fortune albeit in a depressed economy and art market. Scott was certainly a suitable candidate as 'someone best able to do so among those still living who must have known him' but, sadly, did not answer his friend's plea until, eventually, a couple of pages about Holst were published posthumously in his infamous *Autobiographical Notes* of 1892. As well as a glowing opinion of his draughtsmanship, Scott gives an extraordinarily provocative, and so far unique, description of Holst's wife and marriage:

"Holst fell in love, to use an old-fashioned phrase, for a perennial disease, with a wild creature, who led him into ruinous courses. Shortly after my own marriage my wife and I went to a sort of public entertainment, on the opening of the Lowther Arcade, and there we were joined by Von Holst, who introduced a handsome, loudly dressed young woman as his wife. I did not like her, yet she was a noble creature, who wanted not the power of fascination nor the ability to use it. To this lady he accorded what she did not desire - the same freedom of intercourse with the opposite sex that men arrogate to themselves, but she returned him an unconquerable jealousy, and it was said at last kept a stiletto secreted in the sacred hollow of her bodice for his benefit. A sudden illness, however, in 1844, when he was thirty-three, just at the time I left town for Newcastle, saved her from the chance of using it."[2]

It is very frustrating that there is almost nothing else known about Amelia Thomasina von Holst (neé Symmes-Villard) except for our conjectures about her depiction in Holst's paintings and drawings and her disposal of these after his early death. Was she responsible for placing them on long-term display at the West End restaurant favoured by the Pre-Raphaelites, and at the Pantheon gallery close by? If so it ensured, ironically, the best outcome that these commercial failures could possibly have achieved – an extended audience with members of the most important and revolutionary art movement of the nineteenth century!

However Rossetti's diagnosis of the Holst dilemma proved all too correct. His name virtually disappeared from art history until interest in his master Fuseli and *his* extraordinary work snowballed in the twentieth-century and inspired the scholarship necessary to disentangle the work of master and pupil in the 1960s. Since then the gradual reappearance of paintings and drawings onto the market has thankfully allowed a more substantial appraisal of Holst, and his standing within British Romantic art has steadily increased. This recognition is now such that, by 2012, he will be reunited with the Pre-Raphaelite Brotherhood by hanging alongside them at Tate Britain's forthcoming blockbusting *Pre-Raphaelites: Victorian Avant-Garde* exhibition. Thus a sense of poetic justice will be achieved and a circle completed, since William Rossetti reported that members of the Brotherhood regularly dined at Campbell's Scotch Stores in Beak Street because 'it was hung around with pictures by Theodore von Holst.'[3]

It is fortunate that *The Wish* (cat.41) and *The Bride* (cat.42*)*, the two paintings by Holst most admired by Rossetti, are available for public display today whilst so many others remain lost in the oblivion that he so clearly foresaw. The former is to be included in a major European exhibition, *Bohèmes*, in 2012 and the latter, Holst's lovely portrayal of Shelley's fifteenth-century Florentine victim, Ginevra, will be hung in the first gallery of the Tate exhibition and become the harbinger of Rossetti's own 'sensual stunners' which follow.

The 1994 Holst exhibition and catalogue not only answered Rossetti's call for an account and tribute to the artist but also acted as a catalyst in identifying further works, as was hoped. The emergence of works that relate to the influence of Fuseli and Blake and to Holst within the PRB circle has continued.

In a small group of drawings, originally purchased by Imogen Holst from Colnaghi's[4], there is a striking example (cat.20) that shows Holst closely copying one of Blake's most famous designs, the frontispiece to his hundred-page epic prophecy, *Jerusalem*, along with several other motifs. This, of course, leads to the question of Holst's access to Blake's relatively obscure work, which is a fascinating exercise in itself. Names associated in this arena include Sir Thomas Lawrence, William Young Ottley, John Varley, George Richmond and the infamous Thomas Griffiths Wainewright - artist, critic, forger and poisoner.

The next major item to come to light was the Holst sketchbook (cat.34 and Appendix II) owned by Rossetti's friend, the sculptor Alexander Munro. This important discovery was notified to me by the sculptor's grand-daughter, Katharine Macdonald, and eventually achieved a public-unveiling at the Tate's *Gothic Nightmares* exhibition in 2006. The mystery surrounding Munro's acquisition of this sketchbook, namely from whom and whence it came, leads to another fascinating exploration into the network of names connected to the early PRB. As well as Munro and Rossetti, these include Arthur Hughes, Patric Park, William Bell Scott, Millais and Sergeant Ralph Thomas, the collector and dealer.

Additionally two striking paintings, several further drawings and some illuminating and intriguing letters by Holst have appeared in the last few years and they too will be considered.

Art and career

A measure of Holst's exceptional early ability as a draughtsman was his sale of a drawing when only ten years old to Sir Thomas Lawrence, President of the Royal Academy, who paid him three guineas for it. This seminal event took place in the British Museum one day whilst the young artist was copying from the antique statues there. Lawrence's patronage and guidance continued, along with that of his extraordinary friend Henry Fuseli, until the deaths of these elderly Royal Academicians whilst Holst was still a student at the R.A. which he had entered in 1824. Holst's parents had become acquainted with Fuseli some years before this and his tutoring of their gifted protégé left such an indelible mark that it was well over a century later before reliable attributions, to their often seemingly indistinguishable work, could be accepted with confidence.

John Sartain was a student acquaintance and apprentice engraver and included Holst in his *Reminiscences of a Very Old Man*, of 1899:

"Mr Swaine then proposed to me that I should execute any orders that I could procure, and receive a proportion of the profit, an offer that might be called liberal, since by the terms of my indenture all my earnings during my apprenticeship belonged to him. Under this arrangement it was agreed that I should engrave a series of twelve illustrations of Goethe's *Faust*, from designs by Theodore von Holst, the art student I have mentioned as introduced to me by John Varley. The style of Holst's drawing of the human figure was most masterly, firm and grand in outline and free from littleness and triviality of detail, like the contours of Fuseli, whose manner he followed. The proposed series was to be published in quarto form, and to be composed chiefly of etchings imitating his drawings, none of which were wrought up to a finished effect. Only six of the proposed set were ever done, because Holst made no more, but began to introduce other subjects to complete the number. The Wild Huntsman was one of these, and the only one engraved, and the Faust series came to a stand for lack of material. The subjects finished were *Faust in his Study, Mephistopheles and the Student, Faust and Margaret, Margaret in Despair, The Witches departing for the Hartz Mountains*, and *Walpurgis Night*."[5]

For several months in 1827 Holst's parents were away, travelling to relatives in Riga and Germany, leaving their offspring at home to lead relatively independent lives. A letter written to his parents at this time, when Holst was sixteen, informs them that he had just had his first work accepted for the Royal Academy Summer Exhibition, " . . contrary to my thoughts. Likewise I go to Sir Thom Lawrence where I have just come from and am going again Sunday."[6] The drawing accepted by the RA was a repetition from the earlier *Faust* series, *Witches hastening to the Hartzgebirg*: presumably a more finished version than the one reported by Sartain but with its source including all the artist's propensities for the supernatural, macabre and erotic and hence somewhat frowned upon by his parents as 'no agreeable news'. But this was a minor consideration compared to what occurred the following year.

The most powerful illustrations to Faust ever produced were published by Delacroix in 1828. His masterful series of lithographs must have knocked his young English rival sideways and so upstaged him that Holst surrendered this challenge and left his series with Sartain to wither. It is ironic that Delacroix had been relatively unmoved by *Faust* until he saw the operatic version at the Theatre Royal Drury Lane in 1825, after which he wrote of his admiration declaring it to be "the most diabolical thing imaginable . . . theatre can go no further."[7] Holst would have seen this superb show too, and reacted in much the same way, but Delacroix took it further and more quickly than the younger artist and, much as he admired the superb illustrations of the French master, it must have felt a bitter blow to his own plans and ego.

However *Faust* did remain Holst's favourite literary source and a pointer to his aesthetic inclinations towards the poetic dramatisation of subjects rather than any brutal realism of the kind that Delacroix and Goya could depict. Holst's worldly experience did not include war and violence as had many of the European masters. In plate twelve of his series Delacroix shows Margaret's brother Valentin being skewered by Faust's sword. When Holst depicts *Faust*, *Macbeth* or Dante's *Hell* there is a sense of theatrical tension and fancy rather than agonised reality and profundity. This is closer to Fuseli and his dictum that, for the true artist, the depiction of terror is much preferable to horror: for him the moment of highest drama is that just before the fatal sword thrust. For such artists a demarcation line exists between dramatic entertainment and overt documentary - one that Holst rarely stepped over.

In 2001 the London art dealer James Faber showed me a previously unknown gouache drawing that is typical of Holst's daemonic revelleries (fig.8)[8]. It shows an infernal throng sizzling

Fig.8 *Daemonic Revel* c.1830, gouache 18.4x22.8cm., USA collection

with energy similar to the Tate's Faustian painting (1994 cat.57) and the vision of Hell in *Charon* (1994 cat.67) in a private collection. These vigorous designs show Holst letting off artistic steam in a world that few other souls would or could venture into. His debut notice in the inaugural *Art Union* journal admonishes this trait but with much praise:

'There is stuff in him;' Material to form a dozen painters, and all good ones. He seems never to paint until after he has been dreaming: and then before he is half awake. He will not give his mind fair play, but works on as if to be applauded by creations of his own visions was the only recompense he laboured for or desired.[9]

This is the crux of the 'desperate romantic' creative dilemma: the expression of such visions, however creatively fulfilling, must be tempered by substantial harmony with the buying public for commercial success.

Fig.9 *The Cave of Spleen* c.1830, watercolour 19x23.5 cm,, USA collection

In William Bell Scott's opinion:

"His pictures were exactly the kind of pictures for which our school has never even allowed a place, and for which there is no London public at all. They had originality and poetry, but of a purely romantic character, without sentiment: tragic without anything theatrical or transpontine. Besides "Jairus's Daughter" I only remember two: "Mephisto drawing the Wine from the Table," and the "Genius Loci," a pale spirit in a fair landscape. But his sketches were the most astounding – the designs he would have liked to carry out! One of them was "Satan and the Virgin Mary dancing on the Edge of the World"![10]

This was written enthusiastically but decades after Holst's death and with a declared limitation of reference which must include the last mentioned design which seems suspiciously close to the report, in the *Peoples Journal[11]*, of Holst's teenage effort *Lazarus and the Motherpearl Lady dancing on the outside of the World* seen in his studio in 1827. Scott's definition of 'theatrical' also differs from one used by me to describe the graphic composition of drama rather than its depth of visual and emotive power.

Fig.10 William Etty, *The Embarcation of Cleopatra*, RA 1821, Lady Lever Art Gallery

Holst did occasionally exhibit more extreme designs such as *The Deathbed of Lady Macbeth* where the *Athenaeum* critic described how, " . . the writhen brow – the wildly tossed arms – the inverted eye – the foaming lip may not, it is true, overstep what has been witnessed in nature, but belong to one of its most distorted aspects, with which art, we think, has but little concern."[12] But this rare public excursion into daemonic realism by Holst, during the late 1830s, was short-lived. It coincided with the accession of Queen Victoria; the conviction and transportation of his friend Thomas Griffiths Wainewright, and the death of his mother a year later in 1838. After this brief super-satanic period, Holst embarked on a successful remedial course of exhibiting that answered his critics with a prize-winning religious painting, and a series of romanticised female 'stunners' that wooed major collectors and connoisseurs and preceded those by Rossetti some twenty years later.

The darker side of Holst's art was also balanced by his sense of humour. A figure painter greatly admired by many artists and connoisseurs was William Etty - a uniquely single-minded devotee of 'God's most beautiful creation' and of her depiction on canvas. His prolific and lifelong obsession resulted in the production of hundreds of pictures and studies of the nude. However Holst took Etty's more historic and formal picture of *The Embarkation of Cleopatra* (fig.10) as a starting point for a light and humorous theatrical design *The Cave of Spleen* (fig.9), from Alexander Pope's poem *The Rape of the Lock*.[13] In this unusually faithfull depiction of a literary source, it shows Holst having fun with motifs such as the pregnant man, talking teapot and self-portrayal as a serenading troubadour. As a figurative master and former pupil of Fuseli and Lawrence, it would be unusual if Etty had not had some influence on Holst and we can therefore expect more such threads to be discovered.[14]

In a glowing review of the first Holst exhibition[15], the art critic Brian Sewell remarked how strange it was that he could detect no influence by Lawrence on his protégé despite the long-term intimacy of master and pupil. Three years ago this was put to rights with the discovery of Holst's grand *Portrait of Jessy Harcourt* (cat.38). It was painted in 1837 and presumably commissioned by her elder brother, John Rolls, along with the other family portraits and subject pictures by Holst recorded in their family archives. The portrait is composed and executed in a traditional and sensitive manner with the beautiful sitter exposing a long graceful neck, adorned with choker, jewellery and early Victorian dress. It is a particularly important addition to Holst's known oevre, extending our knowledge of his stylistic range. It demonstrates how successful Holst could be with a commission of a more domestic nature as a contrast to the more dramatic designs of his literary output,. Considering his wildly romantic nature it is gratifying to see how such focused application for a major patron could turn out a picture to equal the quality of his masters.

Whilst considering the influence of Lawrence it is pertinent to relate another side of the story that was remarked on by Hall in his obituary of Holst in the *Art-Union*:

"He executed many drawings for Sir Thomas Lawrence, several of which were, we are told, commissioned by George IV, and these were of a class which a youth with very limited means may have been tempted to execute; but the subjects were little to the credit of the President and his royal employer. Who shall say how far the after-career of Holst may have been influenced by this ill-directed patronage?"[16]

There is a dark corner of Regency draughtsmanship which occasionally throws up erotic drawings of this kind; those that have escaped the proprietous consignment to the fireplace which most have suffered. A relatively mild example of such work by Holst was brought to my notice by a dealer in Germany earlier this year, after its rejection as a Fuseli by David Weinglass. It depicts a young courtesan, drawn in a Fuseli-like manner, exposing herself to the viewer (fig.11)[17]. The careful and tentative lines, eccentric coiffure and inscriptions 'Fanny S' and 'June 14 1797' suggest it is a direct copy of a lost drawing by the young artist's master.[18]

Many of the bolder red-blooded artists in history have indulged their fancy in such work including Fuseli and Turner, in Britain, and much of it has been destroyed. The fact that Holst was introduced and induced to such work by the President of the Royal Academy, for the gratification of the Regency court, must have appealed to his youthful salaciousness but intensified his sense of hypocrisy at contemporary values. It goes some way to explain Holst's intense romantic introspection and rejection of convention and, in any age, could be classed as corruption of a minor by his masters.

Perhaps such nurturing in this unusual ambiance may shed light on a recently discovered and most intriguing letter to another ex-student of Lawrence written by Holst on Saturday morning, 21 August 1830 (cat.7):

"What you was so *Kind* to inform my Father with so much *Discretion*, is as Base as it is False. was it I, that forced the girl on you? – or was it not you that beg'd me to introduce you to her? I shall not recapitulate all that I might say, but must add that I despise a Character so devoid of Honour and Gentlemanly feeling"[19]

The addressee was Richard Rothwell, an Irish artist ten years older than Holst who is now best known for his somewhat dull portrait of Mary Shelley in the National Portrait Gallery. But what clash of values does this correspondence throw up? What is so unacceptable about this girl that Rothwell feels he must report to Holst's father? Unfortunately we can only speculate at present, given the sparse documentation available. However a first guess might be that Rothwell unexpectedly found himself face to face with a young courtesan and thought it inappropriate to have been so introduced by a nineteen year old. If so, he would certainly also have disapproved of Rossetti and his friends trawling London's streets looking for their 'stunners' twenty years later.

The following year Holst became the first published illustrator of Mary Shelley's *Frankenstein*. He received the commission, with

Fig.11 *Young Courtesan exposing herself* c.1825-30, pencil and watercolour 21.9x15.5cm., le Claire Kunst, Hamburg.

several others, from Henry Colburn, publisher of the *Standard Novels*. This was a pioneering series of cheap new editions designed to satisfy the huge increase in demand of the reading public brought about by the march of industry and education during the nineteenth century. There were two designs engraved and one of these has now become famous as a result of its reproduction as an early icon of Dr. Frankenstein and his monster (cat.44) a century before its transformation in Hollywood movies.

This was at the very end of the Regency period where a pronounced step down from aristocratic-led social values and artistic taste gave way to that of the rising industrialists and bourgeoisie with a head of steam that signaled the advent of Victorian Britain. The age of Reform ended the post-Napoleonic partying of the 1820s and gave way to the more serious aims of trade expansion and religious moralising. Fuseli had died in 1825 and Lawrence five years later. Holst's two worlds were in transition; one of art and one of society. The flamboyant and extravagant reign of George IV, in which he had been brought up, was being extinguished and so the young artist found himself in this radical new dawn in need of patronage and with ambition to fulfil the artistic and social destiny he must have felt was his due. But how was he to adjust his artistry and behaviour to the new age?

The 1830s were a particularly difficult time for artists. The Victorian economic boom had not yet occurred, patronage and tastes were rapidly changing and figurative art was relatively tame and derivative. The most radical art was being provided by Martin, Constable and Turner in landscape whilst the rest were mostly content to illustrate safe scenes from *Gil Blas*, *Pilgrim's Progress* or the *Bible*. With Holst's exotic Regency foundations, imbibed from Fuseli and Lawrence, and his linguistic advantage, it is not surprising that his taste for German Romantic literature provoked a more advanced and intense pictorial imagery than most of his rivals in England.

The writer and politician Edward Bulwer Lytton appreciated this trait and bought two large paintings from Holst in 1832.[20] Lytton was then ending his short-lived engagement as editor of the *New Monthly Magazine* and had received some enthusiastic prompting about this unusual artist from his assistant, Samuel Carter Hall. One of the paintings was 'The Drinking Scene from *Faust*' (now lost)[21] and the other unrecorded but possibly *Bertalda frightened by Apparitions*, (cat.1994 front-cover)[22] from Motte-Fouqué's fairytale *Undine*, which was recently purchased by the Zurich Kunsthaus and shown at the Tate's *Gothic Nightmares* exhibition.

Sartain added a further reminiscence of Holst:

"He was an intimate acquaintance of Wainewright the poisoner, who was a skilful amateur artist, and in appearance and manners an elegant gentleman. Holst admired him and desired that I should know him, for his true character and heartless crimes had not then, in 1827, been discovered. Holst had always a large quantity of unfinished works on hand, but one thing he did finish was the *Drinking Scene* in Faust, and this was purchased from him by Sir Edward Lytton Bulwer. I have always felt that Bulwer was drawn to Holst all the more because of the known intimacy of the latter with the wretch Wainewright, and much of the information Bulwer thus obtained seems to have been worked up in his novel *Lucretia, or The Children of the Night*."[23]

Thomas Griffiths Wainewright is probably the most enigmatic figure in British art and literary history. An extreme product of the Regency period, his young and accomplished mother had died giving birth to him and he was soon after orphaned and placed in the care of his stern grandfather, Ralph Griffiths, founder-editor of the *Monthly Review*. Wainewright later commented that he never felt his grandfather considered this 'a fair trade'! He subsequently developed only a love of aesthetics and a pathological duty towards his perceived destiny as 'a gentleman' of independent means but, unfortunately, without the necessary financial resources to support it. The diabolical means Wainewright eventually employed to sustain this coveted status forms the basis of narratives by Lytton, Dickens, Wilde and most recently the present Poet Laureate, Andrew Motion.[24]

A friend of Fuseli, Blake and most of the London *literati* in his heyday, Wainewright must have appeared to Holst as the epitome of cultured refinement. So much so that Holst became his rescuer when it seemed that Wainewright was so down on his luck and pocket that it would have been dishonourable and ungentlemanly to refuse him sanctuary whilst on the run from his creditors (actually the police). The fact that he was apprehended, apparently by a chance sighting[25], opposite Holst's house does not imply any stigma of complicity on the part of his friend, but rather that he had no idea of the true nature of the crimes committed.

Just before his trial for forgery in 1837 Wainewright was persuaded to plead guilty (to forging a cheque on the Bank of England) in the expectation of receiving a light sentence. He correctly maintained that this was for money in trust for himself although, under his grand-father's will, he was only entitled to the annual interest. The forgery of his trustees' signatures to gain the capital amount was technically a capital offence and we can only imagine the behind-the-scene conversations about the additional suspicion of his culpability in three untimely family deaths and the related pecuniary gain. Wainewright was shattered to receive his immediate sentence of transportation 'for life' to the penal colonies of Tasmania and his embarkation on the convict hulk *The Susan* which left Portsmouth a few days later. He never returned and died of apoplexy in Hobart in 1847 as, perhaps, the most 'desperate romantic' of all.

On 17 March 1861 Rossetti wrote to Alexander Gilchrist concerning his help with the latter's forthcoming *Life Of William Blake*:

"I have just been reading the greater part of "Janus's" [pseud. Wainewright] Art paper; and really no reading in the world could well be more painful when taken in connection with his life. There is no mistake in their merit. The powers of description are very brilliant and the judgement quite unerring . . . What I wonder have become of the writer's pictures?"[26]

All Wainewright's subject paintings remain lost today but substantial new light has recently been shed on the pictorial output of this extraordinary figure. Wainewright's long lost portrait (fig.12) of his cousin Henry Foss (one of the family to escape his strychnine cull) provides the first example of his brushwork to come to light in England since his last exhibit at the RA in 1825. It is a fine, simple and engaging depiction that, at last, allows us to understand and share William Blake's opinion of his abilities as 'very fine', a comment related by Samuel Palmer when reporting on his visit with Blake to the RA Summer Exhibition in 1824. The appearance of the *Portrait of Henry Foss* now provides an indisputably positive answer to the question of Wainewright's skill as an artist posed by almost all commentators from Rossetti and Swinburne to Wilde and Motion.[27]

As Sartain described, Edward Bulwer Lytton was the first author to weave Wainewright into literary immortality. Lytton was an important figure in nineteenth-century politics, literature and drama. His radical pen entranced voters, readers and theatre-goers and he was a fan of Holst. Their common-ground was German literature, medievalism, romantic imagery, pretty women, pipe-smoking and the occult. In 1834 Holst illustrated a chapter from Lytton's *Pilgrims of the Rhine* (cat.47) and a painting has recently been discovered of *Caesarini and the Soldier in the Forest* (cat.40), from a scene in his novel *Alice: or, the Mysteries,* along with an engraving from it published in an American edition in 1842 (cat.49).

Fig.12 T.G. Wainewright *Portrait of Henry Foss* c.1820-25, oil on canvas 30x25ins, Private Collection

There were two much publicised events in Britain that, at face value, might be expected to have attracted the interest of 'medievalists' such as Holst and Lytton. The first was the Eglinton Tournament that took place in 1839. The recently built rail connection from London to Liverpool and steamship to Glasgow made public travel to the remote Ayrshire venue a realistic venture for the first time in history and a hundred thousand revellers made it a defining Victorian event. It was ostensibly a celebration of medieval chivalry and valour but also included was a large element of support for a conservative backlash against the political reforms of the Whigs and Utilitarians. Despite the torrential rain it was deemed a success and reinforced a cultural tone of valour that lasted throughout the Victorian Age until its demise in the next century, after the unchivalrous Battle of the Somme. Apart from commissioned illustrators it seems to have been largely unattended by historical painters although inspiring subjects of chivalry such as Holst's lost painting of *Front-de-Boeuf*, from Walter Scott's *Ivanhoe*. This was shown at the British Institution the same year and it is worth remarking that at the early age of ten Rossetti may have copied this picture by Holst as a contemporary drawing by him exists of exactly the same subject.[28]

The other national event was for artists - the competition for the decoration of the new Houses of Parliament. It was announced in 1841 and included strict rules of subject, size and medium, which was to be that of the almost unknown 'fresco' technique. Many older established artists declined to take part and the lion's share of the prizes, awarded two years later, went to mostly young unknowns. David and William Bell Scott both entered but failed to make the grade and the latter sympathised with those who had declined "to come before a jury with Sir Charles Eastlake at its head: a jury all biased by the authority of Cornelius and the German revival method of simple outline."[29]

Holst did not compete, probably because it would also have been anathema for him to join a throng bending their skills towards nationalistic propaganda in an unfamiliar medium and particularly at a time when he was enjoying his first and only wave of commercial success. As the competition progressed however, a feeling of being overtaken by the 'rising talent' may have provoked an initiative to reassert his reputation. Towards the end of 1843, and after several drafts, Holst wrote to Bulwer Lytton offering to paint a large, romantic *gratis* portrait of the increasingly famous author and politician such that:

"I could make a grand picture if I might be favoured with a few sittings and one more worthy than those I have seen published with which I am most vexed – I beg to say the picture would be your own - . . "[30]

Lytton replied:

"I am much flattered by your request to take my portrait. But to be painted by a man of your genius who I know will escape all the vulgarities of Mr Chalon. Allow me in conclusion to [tell] you of the pride and pleasure I have felt in your career – for which I always [expect] great things."[31]

Thus the offer was well received, agreed upon, and its progress recorded in a series of letters in the Lytton archives. At his best, a grand depiction of such a celebrated figure would have caused a great stir at the R.A. Summer Exhibition and maintained Holst's momentum with the public but this was sadly not to be. Lytton annotated these letters in 1866:

"The picture referred to is a very bad one, now on the staircase at Knebworth. But he could paint well - He had real genius . . His death appeared to me sudden, . . he dined with me a few days before – But I heard that his [illeg.] had been long affected. He was unhappy in his circumstances – Poor fellow. I mourned for him."[32]

As a fellow romantic, suffering illness himself and a desperately unhappy domestic life, Lytton could certainly sympathise with the tragedy of such seemingly inescapable destiny.

The Pre-Raphaelite Brotherhood

To some degree Bulwer took over the mantle of popular historical novels from Sir Walter Scott and his writing provided a significant source of material for many artists. Both Millais and Rossetti modelled for Holman Hunt as the leading roles in his *Cola di Rienzi Vowing to Obtain Vengeance for the Slaughter of his Brother* of 1848-9. Rossetti's casting as the Italian revolutionary in full cry is perfect for the picture and as a symbol of the PRB battle against stilted figurative art amidst the dramatic backdrop of Europe in revolution at the time.

In the decade leading up to this, Millais, Rossetti and Bell Scott had all become familiar with Holst's paintings and drawings. With his constant craving for recognition, Holst exhibited several paintings each year at the British Institution, the Royal Academy and the Suffolk Street gallery to which the younger artists would have made an annual pilgrimage.

Just after Holst's death and the sale of his remaining works at Christie's, Millais started a Saturday job at the house of the collector and dealer Ralph Thomas who had been a principal buyer there. The teenage Millais was employed for his outstandingly talented draughtsmanship and budding proficiency in oils to produce 'small saleable pictures' for his first patron. As well as being the owner of several paintings by Holst (some unfinished) his collection contained the bulk of Holst's best drawings. The fact that Rossetti reported on this 'legion past numbering' suggests that it was Millais who acted as his informer and possibly introduced him to Thomas and his collection. If so, these two Pre-Raphaelites knew Holst's work better than anyone in history since this key collection remains lost to us today.

If we compare the quantity and prices paid by the two principal buyers of Holst's drawings at his sale[33], John Rolls and Ralph Thomas, it is immediately obvious that, with luck, we have much to look forward to. John Rolls bought most of the first 300 sketches up for sale for £2-4s. Ralph Thomas bought 243 of the later ones for £15-9s. Most of the sketches and watercolours by Holst known to us today are from the cheaper Rolls collection. There were a similar number that went to other buyers or remained unsold. Rossetti asked "what has happened to them?" We continue to wait with bated breath!

Ford Madox Brown mentions Thomas in his diary entry for 12 April 1855.[34] He describes a visit to the Pantheon with his daughter Lucy to see pictures by Mark Anthony 'put there' by Thomas. It is likely therefore that Thomas also put pictures by Holst there too. In the same entry he relates the anecdote of Millais teasing another diner at Campbell's restaurant which led William Rossetti to explain that the PRB went there because it was hung with Holst's pictures.

There is no record of Millais writing about Holst but he was nevertheless an obvious admirer of his talent and of this two clear examples can be cited. Millais's almost unbounded abilities enabled him to change painting styles like a chameleon. In 1846 'Pissaro' was traditional; in 1848 'Cymon' was 'Frostlike'[35], rejected by the RA[36] and the PRB was formed. In 1849 'Isabella' signalled Millais coming of age as a virtuoso innovator and masterful blender of diverse elements. As long ago as 1963 Gert Schiff had noted the similarity of *Lorenzo and Isabella* (fig.14) to Holst's fine watercolour *Les Adieux* (fig.13) which depicts Shelley's fifteenth-century Florentine lovers from *Ginevra*.[37] It is probably such an influence that steered Millais's first Pre-Raphaelite painting in this direction with additional propulsion provided by Holman Hunt and Rossetti.

In 1851 Millais painted his small but powerfully iconic canvas of *The Bridesmaid* (1994 cat. fig.31) with its striking echoes of *The Wish* by Holst. The composition, elements and fatalistic mood are the same and provide a silent PRB homage by Millais to Holst's final successful artistic form, in addition to the more overt ones

Fig.14 J.E. Millais, *Lorenzo and Isabella* RA 1849, Walker Art Gallery

Fig.13 *Les Adieux* 1827, pencil, watercolour and gouache 37x26.2cm., National Gallery of Canada.

expressed by Rossetti's pen and pencil.

The 1868 watercolour of *A Reverie* (fig.16) shows that Millais's admiration was longstanding as he uses the compositional elements of *The Bride* in his design to illustrate a proposed volume of songs by Tennyson set to music by Sullivan. Millais and his wife were regular guests of Lord Lansdowne and would have been familiar with his version of Holst's *Bride* (fig.15) hung *solus* in 'the breakfast room' of his palatial residence in Berkeley Square.[38] The forthcoming Millais catalogue-raisonné by Malcolm Warner is eagerly awaited and may provide further evidence of such influence.

Among recently discovered letters by Holst was one written to his sculptor friend William Behnes Burlowe in 1834:

"It was one of the veritable pleasures I anticipated on my return to London in seeing you, the more so when I heard from my sister of your intended journey, and I called several times but unfortunately when you were from home – should your numerous engagements permit you to waste a farewell hour on Sunday evening I need not say what pleasure your company will give us, we hope to have a little romantic music with a sentimental cup of tea and I shall add a pipe of true Syrian and Damascus – and above all some very pretty women!!! Pray come on the score of ancient friendship."[39]

Fig.15 *The Bride* 1843 (Lansdowne version), oil on canvs, 53½x47¼ins., England, Private Collection

Fig.16 J.E. Millais, *A Reverie* 1868, watercolour (unlocated)

Holst's warm-blooded sensuality, generosity and bravado is evident here in equal degree to that displayed frequently in his draughtsmanship – much like Rossetti. There appears to be the same natural delight in enjoying their 'sensual stunners' and then, perhaps, immortalising them on paper or canvas for later edification and celebration. But there was a difference in their artistic paths, at least in the public domain.

Whilst Holst attracted equal amounts of congratulation and censure for his propensity to exhibit from his fertile imagination without inhibition, Rossetti learned from this and attenuated this side of his art for the sake of a hopefully more fruitful career. Once he teamed up with the young stalwart workaholics, Millais and Holman Hunt, it soon dawned on him that unfettered self-indulgence leads nowhere with the buying public. Rossetti realized that he was caught with the same age-old problem as

Fig.17 D.G.Rossetti, *Seated Man in Renaissance Costume Smoking a Pipe*, Wightwick Manor

Holst: a romantic's most fulfilling and best work must follow the true path of his genius but he still needs to eat. His first exhibited picture then became *The Girl-hood of Mary Virgin* rather than 'Margaret tormented by the Evil Spirit' from *Faust*. We may note in passing though that Rossetti was not averse to propelling members of his entourage to realise such favourite themes, for, under his influence, Walter Howell Deverell exhibited *Margaret in Prison* a few months later at the Royal Academy. Another example of this is Alexander Munro's sensuous treatment of Dante's doomed lovers, *Paolo and Francesca* (fig.20), finished in plaster and exhibited two years later at the Great Exhibition of 1851.

In his teenage years, leading up to the formation of the PRB, Rossetti's reading and graphic output, like Holst, seem to have been dominated by subjects of the supernatural and sorcery. As well as *Faust*, Meinhold's *Sidonia the Sorceress*, Scott's novels and the poems of Poe all provided a feast of imagery that he eagerly turned into a prolific quantity of youthful atmospheric drawings. Many of these found their way into Alexander Munro's collection and form the core of Rossetti's known early *oeuvre*. Among them, but little known, are several sketches featuring very Holstian figures (figs.17, 18, 19). These are now located at Wightwick Manor as part of the growing collection of Pre-Raphaelite art there. It has not been possible to identify any direct copying of Holst's drawings by Rossetti in this group, but the

influence is unmistakable.

As might be expected, both artists' themes and motifs often appear almost interchangeable. Some of the drawings show their stylistic meeting-point and others their divergence. Holst, reared in the wake of his eighteenth-century masters, developed a firm and sensuous line with tonal graduation achieved by cross-hatching and wash. Rossetti, influenced by more contemporary printed illustrations, developed a similarly effective line but often with greater variation of thickness and contrast, adding to the tonal weight, which sometimes approaches that of lithography: Delacroix was a master of this medium and an inspiration to both.

Fig.18 D.G.Rossetti, *Standing Man wearing a Sword*, Wightwick Manor

With regard to exhibited pictures there was one occasion when Holst did accede to criticism of his extravagant subject-matter and painted *The Raising of Jairus's Daughter* (see cat.50), a domestic biblical scene featuring a life-sized cast on a huge canvas. This appeared to answer the call of his critics and was exhibited as, literally, the number one picture at the British Institution in 1841. It won the first prize of 50 gns. and appeased Samuel Carter Hall, editor of the *Art-Union*, who later, to his credit, had it engraved for his *Gems of European Art,* but it failed to sell and was last recorded at the Pantheon as Rossetti described, "relatively weak as a subject of pure dignity."[40] However it was still something of a draw to less demanding members of the PRB circle. In old age Arthur Hughes reminisced, in a letter to Alice Boyd, how he and Walter Howell Deverell, when students, had stood looking at Holst's paintings,

" . . hanging in the Old Pantheon picture gallery in Oxford St., a favourite place of pilgrimage when I was in the Royal Academy Schools."[41] It must also have been the inspiration for Rossetti's older sister, Maria, to compose her poem *Daughter of Jairus* for Lady Isabella Howard, which she presented just after the close of the exhibition.

Fig.19 D.G.Rossetti, *Figure Studies*, Wightwick Manor

A letter from Holst to S.C. Hall (later dubbed 'Shirt Collar' by the PRB for his starchy style of review), in December 1842, joins those recently discovered and describes the problem of its huge size:

"I must apologise for not answering your kind note [?] but I have been in the country with my family. I beg to say that I shall be most happy to lend my picture of "The Raising of Jairus's Daughter" for engraving and only wish to know <u>when</u> and where I am to send it as I shall receive it in a few days from Birmingham. As there is certainly owing to its size some expense in its removal & [?] I venture to [missing] few pounds would be of immeasurable service & will esteem it a favour to hear from you by return of post so that I may avoid the expense and trouble of having the picture at home as it requires to be taken thro' the window."[42]

Holst's smaller picture at the British Institution in 1841, *The Wish* (cat.41), was much preferred by Rossetti. He later based his first widely published poem on its striking and more characteristic image of "a beautiful woman, richly dressed who is sitting at a lamp-lit table, dealing out cards, with a peculiar fixedness of expression."

> Could you not drink her gaze like wine?
> Yet through their splendour swoon
> Into the lamplight languidly
> As a tune into a tune
> Those eyes are wide and clear, as if
> They saw the stars at noon.
>
> The gold that's heaped beside her hand,
> In truth rich prize it were;
> And rich the dreams that wreath her brows
> With magic silence there;
> And he were rich who should unwind
> That woven golden hair.

With the final stanza:

> And do you ask, what game she plays?
> With *him,* 'tis lost or won:
> With *him* it is playing still; with *him,*
> It is not yet begun;
> But 'tis a game she plays with all
> The Game of Twenty-One.

It was published in *The Athenaeum*, 23 October 1852. Four years before this Rossetti had sent a draft copy to his friend 'Mad' (Holman Hunt) just before their founding of the PRB. 'Mad' had queried its mysticism, and Rossetti responded by informing him with slight sarcasm that:

"I am sorry you found a stanza in the Vingt-et-un poem obscure. On referring to the rough copy, I find that it was intended to indicate that state before death when the form of things may be supposed to be lost, while their colours throb, as it were, against the half closed eye-lids, making them to ache with confused lights. I suppose it is dangerous for a man who has not had the advantage of dying to attempt a description of death, and afterward unfortunately there are obstacles in the way. [sentence deleted] In the last line the "game of twenty-one" refers to the title of the poem, which I thought would be sufficient explanation.

"Vingt-et-un" is, as you of course know, a game of cards, at which I have supposed the lady of the picture (personifying, according to me, intellectual enjoyment) to be playing, since twenty-one is the age at which the mind is most liable to be beguiled for a time from its proper purpose."[43]

However notice was taken and by the time Rossetti had exhumed his poems from his wife's grave and published them in 1870, the final stanza had become:

> Thou seest the card that falls, - she knows
> The card that followeth:
> Her game in thy tongue is called Life'
> As ebbs thy daily breath:
> When she shall speak, thou'lt learn her tongue
> And know she calls it Death.

The lightness of romantic youth had by then become the morbidity of crest-fallen middle-age as, perhaps, this symbol of fate by his early hero had prophesised.

The Wish was a seminal source for the PRB. The power of Holst's mysterious *femme fatale* worked as an irresistible charm on Rossetti and Millais who emulated its centrally placed, richly dressed and voluminously-haired female into similar creations of their own. As well as the spring-board for Rossetti's poem it also served as an icon for his large pencil drawing *The Card-Player* (fig.25) and for Millais's famous depiction *of The Bridesmaid* of 1851, noted earlier.[44] *The Water-Witch* (British Institution, 1843 / 1994 cat., fig.32) is another example of Holst's centrally-placed female *provocateurs* that lead to Rossetti's series of sensual 'stunners' of the 1860/70s.

There is one more aspect of Holst's art that should be mentioned with regard to that of the PRB. Haydon recalled in his famous diary that Holst had "felt his want of nature and candidly told me so, but said it was too late, which was a mistake." There are two technical facets that have a bearing here: the first is the problem of short-sight in the Holst family. This is noted in Imogen Holst's biography of her father and in the draft of a letter by Theodor that states "I am miserably in need of an eye glass [or] spectacles to draw in being very short sighted. I use no.7 concave."[45] Hugh Trevor-Roper has described how myopia affects artists:

"When a naturalistic painter is moderately myopic, he will probably see the canvas without difficulty, but not the more distant objects he seeks to reproduce, and he is therefore reduced to painting what he sees, however blurred or distorted a percept it is."[46]

Holst's prescription makes him such a severe case that unaided landscape portrayal would have been impossible. At the British Institution in 1840 he exhibited *A German Tea-garden; sketched from Nature at Dresden* (see cat.8) and *The Art-Union* reviewer, querying the title, clearly identifies this difficulty for the artist. Of course the popularity of later genres such as Impressionism and the Abstract is naturally conducive to artists with such defective vision, as Trevor-Roper goes on to explain.

The second significant technical facet is the development of photography. This was in its infancy in the 1840s but nevertheless provoked an awareness of realism and optics that was at the heart of the 'truth to nature' movement espoused by Ruskin and taken up as the guiding principle of the PRB.[47] Had he lived longer Holst may well have been correct in his self-assessment that it was too late (or even impossible) for him to adapt to this concern for 'realism' and, if so, his technical acceptability to the PRB movement.

In 1994 I speculated that Rossetti might well have approached Holst (had he lived), rather than Madox Brown, to be his painting master before the formation of the Brotherhood. But it may have been an equally short-lived apprenticeship for the future of Victorian painting all too obviously lay in detailed realism rather than extravagant gesture. However this does not denigrate the obvious appeal of Holst to the PRB and particularly his *belles* to Rossetti.

Alexander Munro and Arthur Hughes

Just after Holst's death in 1844, a talented nineteen-year old sculptor, Alexander Munro, left Inverness for London under the wing of the Duchess of Sutherland, the leading aristocratic patron who had purchased *The Bride* from the British Institution two years before. Armed with her introduction Munro was immediately employed to assist with work on Charles Barry's new Houses of Parliament. The work was regular and relatively undemanding and it wasn't long before he began frequenting the studio of another Scottish sculptor, Holst's friend Patric Park. William Bell Scott describes this atelier some years before:

"His abode was near the Hampstead Road, and quickly became the resort of a set greater at laying down the laws of art than at exemplifying them. These have for the most part disappeared, yet some of them were men of mark and character. One of these was Franklin, a saturnine Irishman of breeding and pleasant manners, with a face of the aquiline Cavalier type. He was an illustrator of books, an admirer of the middle ages, with a style of drawing that of the then living Munich school. He was always welcome, and his long pipe was always on the rack with his name attached to it, because Park had a pipe-rack like those in the artist clubs in Munich. Another visitor was Theodore von Holst, whose art was a cross between Retsch and Fuseli, which latter very able inventor anticipated great things of Von Holst. There was an element of simplicity in his composition not to be found in either of the elders."[48]

Park offered studio space to Munro and three years later, after receiving further training with Edward Hodges Bailey, Munro managed to enrol as a student at the Royal Academy. Here he met Rossetti and became a devoted friend and close associate of the PRB but, as with several others, not an official member. Their secretary, William Rossetti, once wrote that, "Gabriel never had a more admiring or attached friend than Munro."[49]

The art world owes a considerable debt to Munro and his family for preserving their large cache of early drawings by Rossetti. A family legend has it that many of these were rescued by Munro

Fig.20 A. Munro, *Paolo and Francesca* 1851, Wallington Northumberland

from oblivion in the studio waste-bin. This was presumably not the near fate of the Holst sketchbook (see cat.34) also in his collection although its acquisition nevertheless remains a mystery.

The Munro-Holst sketchbook was at one time thought to be another youthful outpouring by Rossetti that had been 'rescued' by Munro. However, after comparison with similar drawings reproduced in the Holst catalogue, it became clear that it was actually the work of Rossetti's 'great painter' himself. It contains fifty-seven pages filled with pencil and pen and ink sketches, notes recording paintings or projected paintings with names of patrons, draft letters to Bulwer Lytton and Lord Lansdowne and a title page sketch for a project: 'Faust Fancies by TvH'. Because of its unique importance, further details and sample illustrations from the sketchbook are included in Appendix II.

A watercolour sketch (cat.55) of Holst's painting of *The Bride*, tipped into a commonplace book of Munro's, is also indicative of his regard for the work of the earlier artist. It is freely executed, in reverse, and was therefore probably sketched from memory of the painting in the Duchess of Sutherland's collection. It was mounted in the little volume opposite an inscribed passage from a translation of a poem by Goethe. There are examples of sketches by Rossetti, Millais and Hughes, in Munro's notebooks and we look forward to confirming the authorship of this one too.

As it is now established that both Rossetti and Munro were admirers of and knowledgeable about Holst's work, a further tentacle of influence may be suggested. A favourite and important

Fig.21 A. Hughes, *La Belle Dame Sans Merci c.*1861

subject for all three artists was Dante's portentous tale of the adulterous passion of Paolo and Francesca da Rimini from the fifth canto of *The Inferno*. The universality of Dante's description of the predicament of illicit passion, its discovery and retribution, invoked a sympathetic resonance at the core of Holst's and Rossetti's personas and is consequently reflected in their many variations on this theme. It was also conveyed to, and transformed by, the somewhat less bohemian Munro into his finest sculpture (fig.20).

Holst's lost painting *Francesca da Rimini* appeared in his studio sale and, being unsold, it may well have been one of those appearing later on the walls of Campbell's Scotch Stores restaurant or the Pantheon Gallery and therefore known to the PRB circle. In Munro's Holst sketchbook there are also two sketches of this subject (see Appendix II). The stronger is a lusty depiction of the doomed lovers first embrace which features the murderous husband of Francesca appearing closer to a 'Satan spying on Adam and Eve', but given Holst's eclectic nature, is nevertheless a characteristic depiction. Rossetti's many embracing couples follow on from those by Holst as well as those of the more specific Dante couple portrayed by Flaxman, Ingres, Delacroix and Dyce. With his considerable influence over Munro, it is certain that Rossetti led his sculptor friend in the direction of his favourite embracing-couple, but he let Munro win the race to the exquisitely finished versions of 'Paolo and Francesca' that both artists produced in the 1850s.

A young painter, Arthur Hughes, entered the RA schools in 1847 and the following year met Deverell with whom he writes of visiting the Pantheon Gallery and 'looking at paintings by Theodore von Holst.'[50] He won the silver prize for a drawing from the Antique in 1849 and, in annual steps, met Munro, greatly admired the PRB Journal *The Germ* and was introduced to Rossetti who soon instigated him as another close associate of the circle. From 1852 to 1858 Hughes shared Munro's studio in Upper Belgrave Place, Pimlico and thus also the extended network of the PRB circle.

Given this early background to his art, it is not surprising that echoes of Holst can also be found in Hughes's work. Although blurred by Rossetti's more direct and contemporary influence, Holst's stylistic, supernatural and medieval traits can be seen in both Hughes's early drawings and later book illustrations.[51] The drawings for 'La Belle Dame sans Merci' (fig.21), 'The Rift in the Lute' and 'The Guarded Bower' all show similarities to Holst's depictions of his medieval figures. Hughes's later designs for 'Vanity Fair' (fig.22), 'Phantasies' and 'A Fairy Tale', as late as 1900, similarly display elements familiar in Holst's oeuvre of a more daemonic nature.

Nicknamed 'Cherry' and with a reputation as one of the sweeter of 'the brethren', in both temperament and technique, Hughes's paintings rarely reached the same level of visual impact as those of the leading members of the PRB. However an unusually dramatic excursion, *The Eve of St. Agnes* (Roberts 30.8), comes close to Holst in characteristic features such as the back-lit bedroom scene with strong diagonal window light and the tensely agitated figures which contrast with Hughes's more usual paintings that invoke a mood of sentimental resignation.

Fig.22 A. Hughes, *Vanity Fair* c.1872 (unlocated)

Such indicators shed a little more light on Rossetti's claim for the role of Holst in the progress of nineteenth-century British art, which will, of course, remain far from complete until further works are discovered and assimilated. The late and great PRB scholar, William Fredeman, wrote to me expressing his congratulations on Holst's 1994 entrance onto the modern PRB stage but also that he couldn't 'go as far' as I suggested in proposing him as such a significant influence on its cast.[52] Such reticence is natural of course, but, with a steady accumulation of evidence, the continuing reappraisal of Holst will, I believe, justifiably increase his standing to at least the level acknowledged by Rossetti.

With the ever increasing amount of research, exhibitions, publications and media attention devoted to the PRB it seems appropriate that similar interest in a pre-Pre-Raphaelite increase in proportion. It is heartening to play a small but worthwhile part in the resurrection and reconstruction of the PRB demonstration of human passion, high artistic achievement and its cost. This has most recently been presented by Franny Moyle in her aptly titled book, *Desperate Romantics*, along with the entertaining television drama series of the same title. This bicentenary project attempts to provide an underpinning prequel.

Notes

1. A. Gilchrist, *Life of William Blake*, London 1863, vol.I, p.379.
2. W.Bell Scott, *Autobiographical Notes of the Life of William Bell Scott*, Ed. W. Minto, London, 1892, p.163.
3. W.M. Rossetti, *Pre-Raphaelite Diaries and Letters*, London 1900, p.176.
4. The large album of some 300 drawings collected by John Rolls was eventually sold at Sotheby's, after the death of Lady Shelley Rolls, on 12th June 1959. It was purchased by Colnaghi's and sent to Gert Schiff for analysis at the Schweizerisches Institut für Kunstwissenschaft in Zurich. Dr. Schiff identified several drawings by Fuseli among them and Colnaghi then unbound the album, donated several small groups of drawings to national collections and offered the remainder for sale. For further details see 1994 cat. Appendix II.
5. J. Sartain, *The Reminiscences of a Very Old Man 1808-1897*, New York 1899, p.117
6. See cat.1.
7. J.W. Goethe, *Faust* (with illustrations by Delacroix), London 1977 (ed. M. Marqusee), p.6.
8. The drawing was sold to the London dealer Luca Baroni and subsequently to a collector in the USA.
9. *Art Union*, 1839, p.21
10. Bell Scott, ibid p.164.
11. *People's Journal*, 20 Feb 1847, p101
12. *The Athenæun*, No. 544, 31st March 1838, p.241.
13. See Robert Hallsband, *The Rape of the Lock and its Illustrations*, Oxford 1980. This drawing was once in the collection of the late Professor Hallsband.
14. See cat.42 (*The Bride*) for a possible triangular vector of influence between Etty, Holst and Rossetti and their young women gazing out of window casements. A modern appraisal of the work of William Etty seems long overdue.
15. *London Evening Standard*, 5 May 1994, p.43.
16. *Art Union*, No.64, April 1844, p.87
17. Kindly scanned and notified to me by Karoline von Kügelgen at le Clair Kunst, Hamburg on behalf of the owner.
18. See 1994 cat.nos.21 and 24. Holst could copy Fuseli's drawings with an almost indistinguishable facility and the present drawing undoubtedly adds to the summa of such lost drawings by his master.
19. Purchased by the Trustees of the Holst Birthplace Museum at Bonham's sale, 10th Nov 2009 (lot 58).
20. *Art Union*, April 1844, p.87.
21. This sale was first reported by S.C. Hall in Holst's *Art Union* obituary and may be the 'Scene from Goethe's *Faust*' purchased by Bulwer Lytton from the BI exhibition in 1833 as reported in the *Literary Gazette*, p.106. However this is assumed to be a different picture (1994 cat.54 [i.e. not the 'Drinking Scene']) by Gert Schiff in his *Arts Magazine* analysis in 1980. We now face a quandary over which and how many large paintings by Holst were bought by Bulwer Lytton. In a letter to the artist dated September 9th 1832, Lady Lytton expresses her thanks for the delivery of a first picture and advises delivery of the second as soon as her husband arrives back home. Was it one of these that then appeared at the 1833 BI exhibition, and therefore accords with Hall's total of two, or did Lytton purchase a third?
22. For the record, Martin Butlin's attempt to attribute this painting to T.G. Wainewright, in his 1994 *Burlington Magazine* review, does not appear to have been generally accepted.
23. Sartain, ibid. p.117.
24. See Andrew Motion, *Wainewright the Poisoner*, especially 'Afterword' pp.279ff. Lytton wrote *Lucretia: or, The Children of The Night* (1846); Dickens wrote *Hunted Down* (1860); Wilde wrote *Pen, Pencil and Poison: A Study in Green* (1889). Wainewright fascinates western *literati* with his seemingly unique blend of extreme values towards art and humanity, perhaps because he was deemed to be 'one of us' who went wildly astray. However we do not have to look far into the history of politics and religion to find equivalent sacrifices made to ensure survival of 'chosen ones'. Wainewright was a product of manners not affection and, to him, his existence depended on its upkeep. There was no outpouring of love for nature or fellow creatures, as with so many romantics, but rather a penetrating gaze and measure of the ability of others to depict and engage with their audience. Perhaps 'desperate aesthete' may better describe Wainewright and accord with Mario Praz's suggestion long ago, in *The Romantic Agony*, when he proposed Wainewright as a forerunner of Oscar Wilde. One thing is certain in considering the history of this extraordinary figure, we are provoked to question our own values and their origin too.
25. A. Motion, ibid p.193.
26. W.E. Fredeman, in a letter to the author, 22nd Nov 1996, quotes Rossetti's letter, of 17th March 1861, and provided a draft copy of his extensive Appendix on Wainewright (for his monumental but posthumously published 'Rossetti Correspondence') that had grown from a footnote!
27. I would like to thank my mother-in-law, Sara Burn Edwards, for a most fruitful introduction to the art-valuer, Richard Lane, who notified me of Wainewright's picture last year. Ownership has descended through the Foss family and I am indebted to the present owner for permission to photograph and reproduce it here as Wainewright's 'original oil' publishing debut.
28. This juvenile drawing is reproduced in Fredeman's *A Rossetti Cabinet*, 1991, pl.76.
29. Bell Scott, ibid, vol I p.169.
30. Lytton archives, Hertfordshire County Records Office, D/EK C1/102.
31. Ibid C1/28/21.
32. Ibid C1/103
33. See 1994 cat., Appendix I.
34. W.M. Rossetti, ibid 1900, p.175
35. In the manner of W.E. Frost (1810-77), William Etty's pupil and follower.
36. Holman Hunt records its rejection was as a result of being 'unfinished'. This may raise a smile when we consider the hanging committee faced with such an orgiastic frenzy of topless nymphs from the brush of their star eighteen year old ex-student. Thereafter Millais attenuated the sexual elements of his pictures submitted to the RA with more covert references such as the implied genitalia in *Lorenzo and Isabella* and *Cherry Ripe*. Millais had a naughty sense of humour when aroused.
37. G. Schiff, 'Theodore Matthias Von Holst', *Burlington Magazine*, January 1963, pp.23-32.
38. F.G. Millais, *J.E. Millais*, 1899, I, p.158. Millais must also have known the finer and bolder Stafford *Bride* (cat. 42) so admired by Rossetti.
39. One of 5 letters by Holst to Burlowe in the collection of Mrs. Hildegard Ryals, USA, until 2006 and now unlocated. I am grateful again to David Weinglass for bringing these letters to my attention and for providing photostat copies.

40. See note 1.

41. Cited in L. Roberts, *Arthur Hughes*, 1997, p.12.

42. Author's collection.

43. See M. Browne, 'A Source for Rossetti', *Burlington Magazine* Feb. 1978, pp.88-92. The original 1852 version of the poem is printed in the 1994 cat. p.103.

44. 1994 cat. fig.31 (b&w).

45. See 1994 cat.31 (verso).

46. H. Trevor-Roper, *The World Through Blunted Sight*, London 1997, p.36. An informative introduction to sight defects in artists.

47. A good example of this awareness is provided in Millais's celebrated *Waking* of 1865 (see Smith and Rosenfeld's 2007 Tate catalogue, no.101, with an excellent reproduction). Here Millais uses differential focus to add a superb photo-reality and thus poignancy to his appealing subject who is portrayed slightly 'soft' in contrast to the razor-sharp foreground bedstead and tassled cover.

48. Bell Scott, ibid p.162.

49. Cited in K. Macdonald, 'Alexander Munro' in *Pre-Raphaelite Sculpture* (ed. Read and Barnes) 1991, p.47.

50. See note 30

51. See L. Roberts, *Arthur Hughes* catalogue, 1997.

52. See note 26.

CATALOGUE

OF

THE WHOLE OF THE REMAINING FINISHED

Pictures & Sketches,

IN OILS,

THE WORKS OF THAT INTERESTING AND HIGHLY TALENTED ARTIST,

THEODOR VON HOLST,

Whose Works have excited so much interest from the highly imaginative character of his Compositions, and the vigour with which he embodied them.

THE PICTURES

Comprise the RAISING of JAIRUS' DAUGHTER, the celebrated Altarpiece which gained the Prize at the British Institution; the APPARITION to LORD LYTTLETON; the highly Poetical Work of CHARON; the DEATH of LADY MACBETH; and numerous other Historical and Poetical Subjects and Portraits;

AND NUMEROUS VERY INTERESTING

SKETCHES, IN WATER-COLOURS AND PENCIL, AND CHALKS,

Being first Thoughts for different Compositions:

Which will be Sold by Auction, by

MESSRS. CHRISTIE AND MANSON,

AT THEIR GREAT ROOM,

8, KING STREET St. JAMES'S SQUARE,

On WEDNESDAY, JUNE the 26th, 1844,

AT ONE O'CLOCK PRECISELY.

———◆———

May be viewed two days preceding the Sale, and Catalogues had, at Messrs. CHRISTIE and MANSON's Offices, 8, *King Street, St. James's Square.*

Christie's *Theodor von Holst* catalogue title-page, 1844

Catalogue

The dating of the works is represented in three ways. Where dated by Holst himself the date is shown without brackets; where the date is supported by documentary evidence it is placed in round brackets; where the date is arrived at on the basis of stylistic analysis, it is given in square brackets. The catalogue entry numbers after the '/' refer to those of the 1994 exhibition.

HOLST FAMILY

(All the paintings in this section have been passed down through the Holst family and were donated by Imogen Holst to the Holst Birthplace Museum in 1974. When the Museum became independent ownership of works by Theodor remained with the Cheltenham Art Gallery & Museum but many of these remain on permanent display and are indicated by '*(HBM)*').

1 /1 **Self-Portrait** 1827

> Pen and watercolour, 3½x3¼ins (9.7x7.7cm)
> Drawn on a letter from Gustavus, Theodor and Constantia, to their parents in Riga dated '24. April 1827'
> Prov: Von Holst family by descent
> *Cheltenham Art Gallery & Museum*

This is the earliest known likeness of the artist, aged 16, portrayed on a letter to his parents, at the time he had just finished his first work to be exhibited at the Royal Academy Summer Exhibition:

> Dear Father and Mother / gustav has sent a sketch which I made of myself but it is the worst done of three which I made.
> > when hell links the chain
> > struggling is in vain /
> I've sent a drawing to the Exhibition from Faust which is

admitted luckily contrary to my thoughts. likewise I go to Sir Thom Lawrence where I have just come from and am going again Sunday.

In the same letter the artist's elder brother, Gustavus, recounts how 'Theodore did not wish to send this one, because it looks like a boy. He did another which he intended for you looking like a Man.' This letter, and another dated '21 May 1827' describe how the three younger Holsts have been managing without their parents and Gustavus writes: 'We learn with pleasure that we may look forward to your return to England in a couple of months.'

2 **Sketch of the Artist and Gustavus on the South Downs** 1832

> Pencil and watercolour, 11x21cm
> Drawn on a letter from Theodor to his 'Parents and sisters' and dated 1832
> Prov: Von Holst family by descent
> *Cheltenham Art Gallery & Museum*

This lively and amusing letter describes a visit to the artist's brother who was staying near Eastbourne whilst fulfilling a musical engagement to an aristocratic patron. It describes a windswept walk across the Downs to Brighton and is transcribed in Imogen Holst's biography of her father (*Gustav Holst*, Oxford 1938, pp. 2-4) who was Theodor's great-nephew. Imogen, also noted the comparable sense of humour and romantic spirit shared by these renowned members of her family. A short excerpt demonstrates this:

> I amuse myself with playing the harp a little and when my fingers get sore I get out on the sea shore. There I sit and brood, giving full scope and swing to my Ideas:- no one to disturb me, nothing around but sky, sea and sand. Ah! Quel délice. Then, when the tide is low, I sketch a little on the sands to astonish the oysters, come home, whistle for an hour, read Hoffmann, then get dinner prepared and watch another hour at the window for Gustavus.

(Frontispiece)

3 /2   **Self-Portrait with Brother, Gustavus** [c.1832-37]

Oil on canvas, 29½x24ins (75x61cm)
Prov: Von Holst family by descent
Cheltenham Art Gallery & Museum (HBM)

This is the finest of the family portraits painted by Holst.
Theodor was also an accomplished musician from an early age
and writes of playing the harp, whilst on a visit to his brother
Gustavus, in a letter to his family (cat.2).

A contributor to the *Peoples Journal*, in 1847, vividly describes
a visit to Holst's studio some twenty years earlier: "Even at that
early age he was a confirmed smoker. The youth himself, too,
seemed to belong to a by-gone age, being clad in a kirtle of grey
cloth reaching to the knee, confined at the waist by a leathern
girdle, his dark waving hair falling low on his shoulders, and
his lip slightly shaded by a moustache." Such medievalism, so
prevalent in German and English Romanticism, was a lifelong
feature of Holst's life and art and can be seen in almost all his
self-portraits.

5   **Portrait of a Young Child**   (*c.*1835)

Oil on canvas, 60x49cm
Prov: Von Holst family by descent
Cheltenham Art Gallery & Museum (HBM)

The child depicted is presumably the artist's wild and handsome
nephew Gustavus Matthias, who was born in 1833 and became
an uncle of Gustav Holst. In her biography (*Gustav Holst*, pp.4-
5) Imogen Holst relates how Gustavus Matthias was a talented
and popular pianist, but:

> Unfortunately his charm was not balanced by very much
> discretion, and after appearing at a fancy-dress ball without
> any clothes on, an episode that reduced Cheltenham to a
> horrified silence, he was given a musical appointment in
> Glasgow and told that he need not come back.

Some stylistic influence can be detected here from Holst's early
association with Sir Thomas Lawrence P.R.A.

4   **Portrait of Constantia von Holst** [c.1830-35]

Oil on canvas, 44x33cm (oval)
Prov: Von Holst family by descent
Cheltenham Art Gallery & Museum (HBM)

Constantia (1804-?) was an older sister of Theodor and her
likeness can also be seen in several drawings by her brother (see
fig.5 and 1994 Cat. figs.10 and 17 where she appears as Lilith
and Gretchen respectively).

6 /3   Young Child Riding on a Model Dog [c.1837]

Oil on canvas, 58.4x50.8cm
Prov: Von Holst family by descent
Cheltenham Art Gallery & Museum (HBM)

As above (cat.5) the child depicted is probably Gustavus Matthias a year or two later.

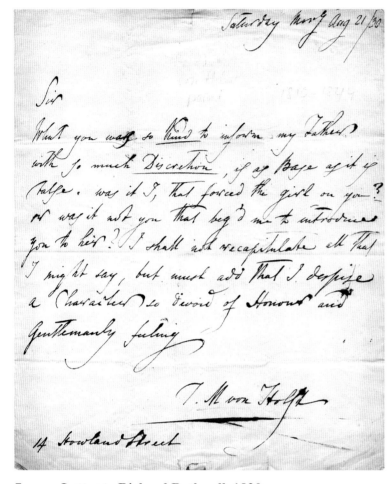

7   Letter to Richard Rothwell 1830

Pen and ink, 20x25cm
Signed one page letter from Holst to the artist Richard Rothwell (1800-68)
Prov: Bonhams, 21 August 2009 (58)
Holst Birthplace Museum

This letter has recently been purchased by the museum and is Holst's only known correspondence with Rothwell. The message and indignant tone are highly intriguing and are considered elsewhere (see p.19). Rothwell was also a student of Sir Thomas Lawrence and his best known work is the portrait of *Mary Shelley* (1840) now in the National Portrait Gallery. Holst became the first published illustrator of Mary Shelley's seminal novel *Frankenstein*, in Colburn's *Standard Novels* edition of 1831 (cat.44).

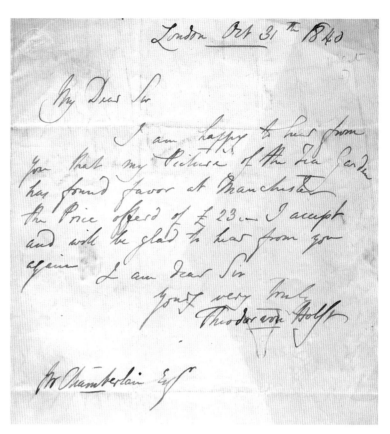

8   Letter to William Chamberlain 1840

Pen and ink, 23x19cm
Signed one page letter from Holst to the Director of the Royal Institution, Manchester, dated 31 October 1840.
Prov: Purchased from John Wilson, March 2010.
Holst Birthplace Museum

This is another recently discovered letter, purchased by the museum, and states:

> I am happy to hear from you that my picture of the Tea Garden has found favour at Manchester. The price offered of £23 I accept and will be glad to hear from you again.

A German Tea Garden; sketched from Nature at Dresden was first shown at the annual exhibition of the Society of British Artists, Suffolk Street, (no. 415) in April 1840. It was reviewed in *The Art-Union* as "A striking but not a pleasing picture; it is full of talent as are all the productions of this artist's pencil, but even in his copies of facts (he describes this as "sketched from nature,") he seems never to let his imagination rest" (p.54). In the September issue (p.146) the picture was reported in the Exhibition of the Royal Manchester Institution. In January 1841 (p.13) it was reported as sold but further research is required to track down its subsequent provenance. It does not appear in the collection of the present Manchester Art Gallery.

The problem of severe short-sight affected Theodor, as well as his great-uncle Gustav, and the consequent inclination to express inner vision, rather than 'nature', goes some way to explain the intensity of their romanticsm.

DRAWINGS

9 /6   **Caricature of the Artist as a Winged Devil Smoking
a Pipe** (1832-35)

Pencil, pen and brown ink, 8¼x6⅜ins (21.2x15.3cm)
Watermark '1832'
Prov: Rolls Album; Colnaghi; Christopher Powney
England, Private Collection

Holst caricatures himself in a very similar pose to that painted in
A Dream after Reading Goethe's Walpurgisnacht (See 1994 cat.
frontispiece) where he again gives the principal subject his own
likeness.

10 /26   **Psyche Attended by Invisible Maids** [c.1825-35]
(Apuleius, *The Golden Ass*, Cupid and Psyche I)

Pencil, 7¾x5¾ins (19.8x14.5cm)
Inscr. 'T Von Holst 1844'
Prov: Rolls Album; Colnaghi; Christopher Powney;
John P.Hardy
England, Private Collection

The soft and delicate rendering of this drawing recalls the
style of Thomas Stoddard RA (1755-1834) although its overt
sensuality is more pronounced than that of the older artist.

Psyche, after acceding to the command of Apollo's oracle,
apparently to prepare her to become the bride of some dread

immortal, is, instead, transported to an enchanted palace and
finds herself attended by the voices of invisible maids, who
mysteriously prepare her for her first night with the unsuspected
Cupid. The lines illustrated are:

> First she found her bedroom and dozed off again for awhile,
> then she went to the bath, where invisible hands undressed
> her, washed her, anointed her and dressed her again in her
> bridal costume. (R.Graves)

11 /48   **Mephistopholes and Student in Faust's Study**
(c.1825-26)
(Goethe, *Faust* I, VII)

Pencil, 8½x7⁵/₁₆ ins (22x19cm)
Inscr. '2 | Von Holst'
Watermarked 'J.Whatman 1825'
Prov: Rolls Album; Colnaghi; Christopher Powney
Cheltenham Art Gallery & Museum

This shows the influence of Retzsch's *Faust* outline designs
although his series did not include an illustration for this second
scene in Faust's study. Holst's design includes a subtle sexual
innuendo in the form of the phallic laboratory flask and student's
protective stance. The engraver John Sartain (see p.16) lists this
subject as one of the proposed Holst *Faust* series he was to have
engraved in 1826 and so it is likely to be a sketch for that design.

The arrival of a new student interrupts the conversation of the
ageing and disillusioned academic, Faust, with the scheming

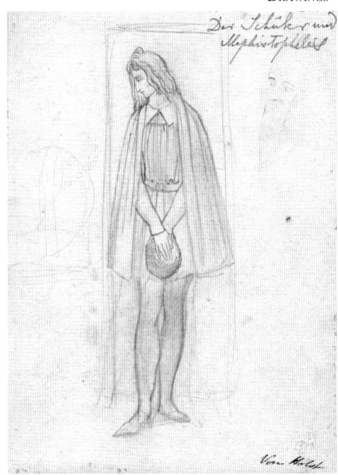

Mephistopheles, who promptly impersonates the former and exposes the Student to some of his alternative philosophy:

> Now, you're still fairly young and strong
> And, I dare say, a bold lad too;
> Just let self-confidence carry you along,
> And others will have faith in you.
> Learn, above all, to handle women! Why,
> In all their thousand woes, one sure
> And certain cure
> Will end their endless sob and sigh!
> With a polite approach you'll put them at their ease,
> And they'll be yours to treat just as you please.
> A door-plate helps; she'll think: Now he
> Has a superior degree! (trans. D. Luke)

12   The Student in Faust's Study (c.1825-26)

Pencil 8¾ x6½ ins. (22.2x16.5 cm)
Signed 'Von Holst' and inscribed in pencil 'Der Schuler und Mephistopheles'
Prov: Rolls Album, Colnaghi; Imogen Holst
Aldeburgh, Britten-Pears Library

This is a study for the preceding entry (cat.11). The figure of the student here is similar to the outline style of the popular German illustrators of the period and leads to the later comparable drawings by Rossetti, Millais and Hughes (see fig.21).

13   The Confessional [c.1825-30]

Pencil, pen and brown ink 22.1x16.7cm
Insr 'T Von Holst 1844' and, by the artist, 'The Confessional'
Prov: Rolls Album, Colnaghi
England, Private Collection

This is probably a penitent Margaret anxiously sharing her burden of guilt concerning her liaison with Faust. In style and size it belongs with the early Faust drawings along with cats.11,12 and possibly 25.

15 /33 **A Man with a Club-Foot Talks to a Young Woman Kneeling at His Side** [1827-35]

Pen and pencil, 6³/₈x7³/₄ins (16.3x19.9cm)
Inscr. 'T Von Holst 1844'
Prov: Rolls Album; Colnaghi; Paul Grinke; Alister Mathews
England, Private Collection

An identification with Heinrich Von Kleist's comedy *The Broken Pitcher* is possible when, in scene 12, the young Eve recounts how the club-footed Justice Adam attempted to seduce her by tricking her into believing he could save her lover, Ruprecht, from a fictitious drafting into military service.

16 **Mephistopheles with the Rejuvinated Faust and a Courting Couple and Child** [1828-35]

Pencil and watercolour, 8½x12¼ins (21.5x31cm)
Paper watermark '1828'
Prov: Rolls Album; Colnaghi; Sotheby's 13-8-80 (38); Phillips sale (right half of drawing only)
England, Private Collection

The recent history of this drawing is remarkable for its unfortunate mutilation in the early 1980s. After appearing at Sotheby's complete it was cut in two and approximately ¾ inch trimmed away from the centre and Faust's left foot erased. The right hand portion was then offered for sale at Phillips. A somewhat clandestine comment subsequently revealed that the other half was available and was also duly purchased. Happily this divorce was annulled and the two halves brought together again but only at the cost of leaving a sad gap of evidence.

[Illustration is prior to the mutilation]

17 /68 **A Nursing Mother** [1835-43]

Pencil, 7³/₁₆x6⁷/₁₆ins (18.3x16.4cm)
Inscr. 'Von Holst'
Prov: Rolls Album; Colnaghi; Christopher Powney
England, Private Collection

This provides a pleasant contrast to the more dramatic and fantastic subjects that tend to dominate Holst's *oeuvre*. The style of this drawing beats a path to Millais's Germanic outline drawings of the late 1840s. Millais's first patron was Sergeant Ralph Thomas, the owner of a large collection of drawings by Holst. Rossetti recalled this collection years later, when writing about Holst, and it is reasonable to suppose that he and Millais picked up some hints from the draughtsmanship of the older romantic.

18 /34 **Figure Studies** [1825-35]

Chalk and pencil, 7³/₈x10⁵/₈ins (18.8x27.1cm)
Inscr. 'T Von Holst'
Prov: Rolls Album; Colnaghi; Christopher Powney;
Caroline Stroud
England, Private Collection

Fig.23 William Blake, *Jerusalem* frontispiece.

20 **Sheet of Figure Studies after Blake** [1825-30]

Pencil and pen 7³/₄x12 ins (20x30.7cm)
Insribed in pencil 'T Von Holst'
Prov: Rolls Album, Colnaghi; Imogen Holst
Aldeburgh, Britten-Pears Library

19 /35 **A Man in Classical Dress is Terrified by a
Menacing Figure Squatting on a Globe
Holding a Glowing Orb** [1825-35]

Pencil, 9x11¾ ins (22.8x29.5cm)
On the back sketches of two male figures and a bearded
man.
Prov: Rolls Album; Colnaghi; Christopher Powney
England, Private Collection

The manner of this sketch is reminiscent of early neo-classical
drawings by William Blake but the subject remains unknown.

This important sheet of studies shows Holst copying figures
from William Blake's epic prophetic book *Jerusalem* and
was the subject of an article by the present author in *Blake
an Illustrated Quarterly*, Winter 1995/6, pp.78-81. Although
Holst was previously known to have used motifs freely taken
from Blake this was the first time that the actual copying of a
major Blake work had to come to light. It adds further weight
to Rossetti's claim of Holst 'as a link of some consequence'
between Blake, Fuseli and the Pre-Raphaelite circle.

It is one of four drawings by Theodor given to Benjamin Britten
and Peter Pears by Imogen Holst after her return from a trip to
Venice in 1964 where Britten was working on *Curlew River.*

21   Outline sketches of grotesque figures and caricatures (c.1833)

Pencil, 21x32.8cm
Inscr. 'T Von Holst' with male figures on verso.
Paper watermarked with Brittania emblem
Prov: Rolls Album, Colnaghi, Christopher Powney
England, Private Collection

This sheet of grotesque and caricature studies is similar to no.65 in the 1994 Cat. which is inscribed 'Eastbourne 183[3]'. The figure of Dante, lower left, identifies the literary source.

Fig.24 R.Westall, *Faust preparing to Dance with a Young Witch* (detail) RA 1831 London, Odin's Restaurant

Combining Holst's interest in music and art, this is the infernal cello-player seen in Richard Westall's exotic painting *Faust Preparing to Dance with the Young Witch* exhibited at the RA in 1831 (fig.24). The attribution is based on stylistic grounds.

22   Version of Richard Westall's Infernal Cello-Player (1831-35)

Black and white chalk on pale blue paper, 13½x10¼ins (34x26cm)
Prov: Portobello Market stall 1970s
England, Private Collection

23   Portrait Sketch of a Young Man   [1835-40]

Pencil on card, 33.8x16.5cm
Inscr. with a note naming other artists at top of card.
On the back sketches of heads and woman wearing a crown.
Prov: Rolls Album; Colnaghi; Christopher Powney
England, Private Collection

An accounting note above the portrait sketch refers to Pickersgill, Dadd and Park and so this may be a sketch of one of the circle of artists who Holst met regularly at the studio of the sculptor Patric Park and at the house of the influential editor/publisher Samuel Carter Hall in the 1830/40s.

24 A Milkmaid and her Lover [1832-36]

Pencil, 27.3x36.7cm
On the back sketches of limbs and heads.
Prov: Rolls Album; Colnaghi; Christopher Powney
England, Private Collection

This is possibly a sketch related to Holst's now unlocated painting of the same subject which was sold at Christie's in 1972 along with *The Fairy Lovers* (1994 cat.55) purchased by the Tate.

25 Seated Couple in Medieval Costume Embracing [1825-30]

Pencil, pen and watercolour 7½ x 6 inches (19 x 15.5 cm)
Signed 'Von Holst' in ink and inscribed in pencil 'white', 'violet'
Prov: Rolls Album, Colnaghi, Abbott and Holder
London, Scott Thomas Buckle

The couple embracing here is stylistically consistent with a represention of the seduction of Margaret by Faust.

26 Young Woman Kneeling on Cliff Edge Pleads to Flying Figures [1827-35]

Pencil, 9 x 6 inches (25 x 17.5 cm)
Inscr. 'Von Holst'
Prov: Rolls Album, Colnaghi, Abbott and Holder
London, Scott Thomas Buckle

The literary source for this striking design is unknown. The leaping and flying figures are derived from those by Fuseli and Blake.

**27   A Woman with a Sword gesticulates before a
Saintly double holding a Cross.** (1831-35)

Pencil, 33.8x16.5 cm
Inscr. 'T Von Holst' and 'Infidels' on paper watermarked
'J Whatman 1831'.
On the back studies of heads and a witch astride a flying
owl.
Prov: Rolls Album; Colnaghi; Christopher Powney
England, Private Collection

An unknown dramatic subject.

**28   A Distraught Nude Man is alarmed by an Egyptian
Mummy and two Portrait Sketches of a Young
Woman** 1833

Pencil, 31.8x38.6cm
Inscr. 'Eastbourne 1833'
Prov: Rolls Album; Colnaghi; Christopher Powney
England, Private Collection

Both portrait and dramatic sketches are of unknown subjects
but were presumably drawn on one of the artist's trips to visit
his brother as described in a letter written from Eastbourne the
year before (see cat.2). The male figure is similar to those in
Flaxman's illustrations to Dante (*Inferno* XXIV).

**29 /53   Sketches of Lady Macbeth with a Dagger, and
a Female Dancer** (1830-35)

Pencil on laid paper, 9³/₈x8½ins (23.8x21.7cm)
Inscr. 'Von Holst' with a watermark 'J RUMP 1830'
On the back: Pencil sketches of heads and a male torso
with an inscription by the artist, 'Rainbow Colours/
Violet/Emerald Green/Yellow/Lake/Blue' and 'Theodore
Rombou[tz?]' beneath a possible self-portrait
Prov: Rolls Album; Colnaghi; Christopher Powney
England, Private Collection

Lady Macbeth and gyrating female dancers were both favourite
subjects for Fuseli and Holst's dancer is perhaps derived from
one by his master and certainly relates to a similar figure, in
reverse, of Helen in Holst's painting of *A Scene from Goethe's
Faust* (1994 cat.no.54).

30 **A Furtive Man in Renaissance Costume stoops to pick something up** [1830-35]

Black, brown and white chalk, 15.8x14.4 cm
Prov: Rolls Album; Colnaghi; Christopher Powney
England, Private Collection

31 **A Distraught Man Raises his Hands to his Head** [1830-35]

Pencil, 6¼x5¾ins
Inscr. 'Von Holst'
Verso male figures drawing daggers and lines from a letter draft.
Prov: Rolls Album, Colnaghi
Cheltenham Art Gallery & Museum

A striking but unknown subject.

32 **A Distraught Young Woman Rests her Head in her Left Hand** [1830-40]

Black chalk, 7x3¾ins (17.9x9.5cm)
Prov: Holst family by descent
Cheltenham Art Gallery & Museum (HBM)

With its almost lithographic quality, the broad and bold style of this attractive drawing is unlike any others known at present by the artist. It has an echo of Fuseli such as his early lithograph *Evening thou bringest All* (fig.25) commisioned by Phillipp André to demonstrate the new medium then called 'polyautography'.

Fig.25 H.Fuseli, *Evening thou bringest All*, 1803, lithograph

33   Sketch of a Tree Trunk [1830-35]

Pencil, 7½x6ins
Signed in ink 'T Von Holst'
Prov: Rolls Album, Colnaghi, Imogen Holst
Cheltenham Art Gallery & Museum

An unusual subject for Holst that shows an inclination to overcome his difficulty with seeing and depicting nature - a problem shared with many other short-sighted artists.

MUNRO-HOLST SKETCHBOOK   (1834-44)
The displayed pages are 34v/35:

34   A Flying Nude Couple watched by a Winged Devil / Head of a Horned Devil
pencil and pen / pencil, pen, black chalk and yellow wash.
The sketchbook contains 57 double-sided pages with designs and notes in various media, 8⁷/₈x6⁵/₈ins (22.5x17cm)
Exh: Tate Britain *Gothic Nightmares* 2006 (73)
Prov: Alexander Munro and by family descent.
London, Katharine Macdonald

This is the only known Holst sketchbook and it has been passed down through the family of the sculptor Alexander Munro (1825-71). At one time it was thought to have been by Rossetti, who was a close friend of Munro, but comparison with drawings in the 1994 Holst catalogue finally established its correct author. It is an important discovery and includes striking designs in pen and pencil, notes of planned and extant pictures and patrons, a proposed series of 'Faust Fancies by TvH' and draft letters to Holst's patrons, Edward Bulwer Lytton and Lord Lansdowne, written the year before the artist's death. Because of its significance further description and illustrations are given in Appendix II.

The flying couple in the displayed design may represent Dante's 'Paulo and Francesca' and the striking horned devil is a variant of the similar design in cat.21.

PAINTINGS

35 /51   **Clarissa Harlowe in the Prison Room of
the Sheriff's Office** (c.1833-37)
(S.Richardson, *Clarissa*, Letter CVI)

Oil on lined canvas, 30x25" (76.1x63.2cm)
[This is possibly the *Weeping Girl*
recorded in the Rolls archives]
England, Private Collection

Holst has copied the basic composition from
Charles Landseer's painting of the same subject
shown at the RA in 1833 (1994 cat.fig.36) and now
at Tate Britain. This may have been commissioned
as a variant on Landseer's composition for Holst's
patron, John Rolls, since a picture of a *Weeping
Girl* by the artist appears in the archives of his
estate. If this is so, the interest of the Rolls family
in the theatre may also be reflected in Holst's
modifications such as the floorboards being turned
to reinforce the stage effect along with the unusual
'footlights' illumination. Holst has reduced the
composition to its essential elements whilst also
improving Clarissa's eyeline towards the spectator,
thereby intensifying the viewer's emotional
response. The illustrated lines are:

> When I surveyed the room around, and the
> kneeling lady, sunk with majesty too in her
> white flowing robes (for she had not on a hoop)
> spreading the dark, though not dirty, floor,
> and illuminating that horrid corner; her linen
> beyond imagination white, considering that
> she had not been undressed ever since she had been here; I
> thought my concern would have choked me. Something rose
> in my throat, I know not what, which made me, for a moment,
> guggle, as it were for speech: which, at last, forcing its way,
> Con-con-confound you both, said I to the man and woman, is
> this an apartment for such a lady?
> And could the cursed devils of her own sex, who visited this
> suffering angel, see her, and leave her, in so damned a nook?

36 /60   **Bertalda Frightened by Apparitions** [c.1830-35]
(Friedrich de la Motte-Fouque, *Undine*, ch. 13)

Oil on canvas, 31¼x24¼ins (79.5x61.5cm)
Prov: Sotheby's 13 July 1988 (95), bt Heim; Anthony
Mould
Exh: Tate Britain *Gothic Nightmares* 2006 (109)
Cheltenham Art Gallery & Museum (HBM)

Purchased by Cheltenham Art Gallery in 1996 this fine portrayal
of one of Holst's favourite scenes from Romantic literature
clearly displays the influence of Fuseli. The composition, based
on crossed diagonals, is compact, economic in its spatial depth
and emphasized by an architectural detail bordering the right
side. It shows a more youthful, finely coloured and sensuous
treatment than the canvases of Fuseli, but Holst adopts the
pointing fingers and intimidating background figures of his
master to heighten the sense of vulnerability and, in this case,
eroticism of Bertalda that achieves a similar dramatic tension.

The larger variant of this subject by Holst (featured on the cover
of the 1994 catalogue) has now been acquired by the Kunsthaus,
Zurich so bringing pupil and master together again in this great
Swiss collection. Neither painting is identifiable in contemporary
records which indicates that they were probably sold from the
studio or were commissioned works.

Baron Friedrich de la Motte Fouqué published his classic fairytale, *Undine*, in 1811. It relates how an adopted elemental water-
sprite (Undine) has been brought up by an old fisherman and
his wife and falls in love with a knight (Huldbrand), with whom
she marries, and by this union acquires a soul. Undine and
Huldbrand travel back to the city where the knight's first love,
Bertalda, is living with her foster-parents. Here it is discovered

that Bertalda is the long-lost daughter of the fisherman and his wife. Undine and Bertalda go with Huldbrand to his home, Ringstetten Castle. While they are staying there Huldbrand falls in love with Bertalda again. The lines illustrated are:

> Undine gave way in melancholy resignation . . . What still further disturbed social life in the castle were all sorts of strange apparitions, which confronted Huldbrand and Bertalda in the vaulted passages of the fortress . . . The tall white man, in whom only too well Huldbrand recognised (Undine's) Uncle Kuhleborn, and Bertalda the ghostly fountain-man, often rose menacingly before them both, but particularly in front of Bertalda, so that already once or twice she had been made quite ill with the terror of it, and often determined that she would quit the castle. (trans. E. Gosse)

37 /63   **Macbeth, Banquo and the Witches** (c.1830-37)
(Shakespeare, *Macbeth*, IV, I)

Oil on canvas, 34½x45ins (87.6x114.3cm)
Exh: *Fuseli painter of Shakespeare*, Parma 1997 (85)
Prov: Sergeant Ralph Thomas (his sale, Phillips, 2 May 1848, lot 38{13gns}), Sterne Gallery, London 1976
England, Private collection

This is probably Holst's Royal Academy picture of 1837 which was accompanied in the catalogue by a quote from an earlier scene on the Heath, presumably in error. The composition is somewhat theatrical and exhibits many characteristic traits including the artist's own likeness given to Macbeth. Also of iconographic note are the pointing witch and flying moth, favourite motifs of Fuseli, and the crescent moon, owl, skulls and skeleton all used previously in a similar manner by the artist. Frederick von Raumer, in his survey of *England in 1835* (I, pp.197-199), describes a highly melodramatic performance of *Macbeth*, staged at Covent Garden in April 1835, with the parts of the three Witches being played by men.

In Shakespeare's tragedy Macbeth, spurred on by his ambitious wife, has murdered Duncan, contrived that of Banquo, and crowned himself King of Scotland. Haunted by the ghost of the latter he has come to the cavern of 'the weird sisters' to seek his destiny. They in turn have conjured up a series of apparitions the last of which consists of eight Kings with the ghost of Banquo following. The lines illustrated are:

Macbeth. Thou art too like the spirit of Banquo; down!
    Thy crown does sear mine eye-balls:- And thy hair,
    Thou other gold-bound brow, is like the first:-
    A third is like the former:- Filthy hags!
    Why do you show me this? - A fourth? - Start, eyes!
    What! Will the line stretch out to the crack of doom?
    Another yet? - A seventh? - I'll see no more:-
    And yet the eighth appears, who bears a glass,
    Which shows me many more; and some I see,
    That two fold-balls and treble scepters carry:
    Horrible sight! - Ay, now, I see, 'tis true;
    For the blood-bolter'd Banquo smiles upon me,
    And points at them for his. - What is this so?
I *Witch*. Ay, sir, all this is so:- But why Stands Macbeth thus
    amazedly? -

38   Portrait of Jessy Harcourt
1837

Oil on canvas, 125.x100cm
Inscr. (old label rear of stretcher) identifies the sitter and includes biographical details.
Prov. Clevedon Auctions, Bristol, 6 December 2007 (232)
England, Private collection

Painted in the year of Queen Victoria's coronation, this fine and traditional portrait demonstrates how successful Holst could be with a domestic subject when commissioned by an important patron. The time spent at the studio of Sir Thomas Lawrence, as a teenager, is evident here where the grace of the sitter is emphasized by the plain background and set off by the simple arrangement of an orchid (exoticism) and rose (love) in a slim vase and small decanter which impart a phallic suggestion. The addition of a shield and carved date lend an archaic timelessness to this depiction, which is one that widens the beam on Holst's *oeuvre*.

Jessy (1809-42) was a younger sister of John Rolls of The Hendre, Monmouth, a wealthy and cultured landowner who became Holst's most avid patron (see 1994 cat. Appendix II). The Rolls family had built a theatre in the grounds of their estate, which was frequented by many luminaries from the London stage including William Macready who was Bulwer Lytton's partner in their smash-hit plays in London in the late 1830s. In 1833 Jessy married George Simon Harcourt who became High Sheriff and M.P. for Buckinghamshire from 1837-41. Holst exhibited two further portraits of the family at the Royal Academy in 1841: *Mrs. Harcourt and Child* (217) and *George Simon Harcourt Esq., MP* (40) both of which remain lost. Tragically Jessy died the following year and the exceptionally long letter of bereavement from her husband to his brother-in-law is in the family archive at Gwent County Records Office, Cwmbran (D361 F/P 4.23).

Jessy was the great-aunt of the pioneer aviator Charles Rolls (1877-1910) the co-founder of the automobile manufacturer Rolls-Royce.

39 /73   Hero and Leander (1830-40)
(Schiller, *Hero and Leander*)

Oil on canvas, 50½x40ins (128.5x101.5cm)
Prov: Christie's 12th April 1991 (37)
England, Private Collection

Hero and Leander and *The Treasure-seeker* were both shown at the Royal Academy in 1840 but, according to the *Art-Union*, were hung so high they could hardly be seen let alone reviewed. This was the principal focus of the annual complaints of reviewers and artists of exhibitions of the period and goes some way to explain why both pictures remained on the artist's hands until his death. A feature in common with *The Treasure-seeker* concerns the evidence of a previous composition beneath the present one. Jon Benington has pointed out the motif of a girl's head, characteristic of the artist, which is just visible to the right of that of Leander, with an orientation at right angles to the present work and of smaller scale. This is all that can be detected at present and further examination, possibly by X-ray photography, may be required to reveal additional hidden detail. The fact that Holst resorted to such over-painting reflects, perhaps, the dire financial problems that he and many of his contemporaries often faced.

These two paintings also share a distinctly Fuselian manner which seems stronger than in other works by Holst at this time and may point to their earlier gestation. Another treatment of this subject by Holst has recently come to light in the form of the fine watercolour (fig.7) which is now in a collection in the USA. Holst's infamous friend T.G. Wainewright edited an edition of Marlowe's *Hero and Leander* published in 1820.

The classical legend related by Musaeus has been treated by several other writers including; Schiller, Grillparzer, and Hood. Holst may have been familiar with all of these but Schiller's ballad seems to come closest to his illustration and we use here the translation by Holst's patron Edward Bulwer Lytton. The legend relates how Leander meets his lover Hero, a beautiful young priestess, illicitly every night by swimming across the Hellespont straights. One night a terrible storm overwhelms Leander and he is drowned. The distraught Hero, in despair, hurls herself into the sea after her lover. The lines illustrated are:

Still in that theft of sweet delight
Exalt the happy pair;
Caress will never pall caress,
And joys that Gods might envy,
bless
The single bride-night there.
Ah! never he has rapture known
Who has not, where the waves are
driven
Upon the fearful shores of Hell,
Pluck'd fruits that taste of Heaven!
(trans. Sir E.B. Lytton)

**40   Caesarini and the Soldier
         in the Forest** (c.1838-41)
         (E.B. Lytton, *Alice; or, The
         Mysteries*, Bk.8, Ch.5)

Oil on canvas, 76.1x63.2cm
Engraved: See cat.49
London, Scott Thomas Buckle

This recently discovered painting adds
to the Holst–Lytton connection in both
patronage and artistic terms. It displays
a teutonic intensity that Holst's famous
novelist patron much admired. It is also
the trait that was regularly complained
of by reviewers when commenting
on Holst's rejection by the buying
public. They regarded such vivacious
romanticism as eccentric compared to
the tamer conventionality of the scenes
that they were more accustomed to.

The scene selected is untypical of the
novel but entirely suitable for Holst with
its darkly romantic forest setting and
dramatic fire-lighting which echoes the
masterly incandescent effects of Joseph Wright of Derby (1734-
97). Holst adds his own characteristic touches of prominent star,
moonlit background and overseeing owl to heighten the tense
atmosphere. It is tempting to speculate if Holst had witnessed
a theatre scene like this as he probably did before his rendering
of *Preciosa*, from the Weber-Wolff opera, shown at the Royal
Academy in 1841 (536) but which is now lost.

The painting does not appear in exhibition lists or other
documentation apart from the engraved illustration of it in
Harper's collected edition of Lytton's novel published in the
USA in 1842 (cat.49).

Alice is the sequel to *Ernest Maltravers*, originally published the
year before, in which can be found significant autobiographical
traces of Lytton himself as the hero attempting to rescue his
much desired and innocent damsel in a wicked and conspiring
world. In this dramatic scene the distraught Italian poet,
Caesarini, and a deluded army officer have escaped from a
lunatic asylum near Paris. They have lit a fire and begun to argue
prior to a fight which is broken off as they hear the approach of a
distant search party. The lines illustrated are:

> On a little mound, shaded by a semicircle of huge trees, sat
> the Outlaws of Human Reason. They cowered over the blaze
> opposite to each other, the glare crimsoning their features.
> And each in his heart longed to rid himself of his mad
> neighbour; and each felt the awe of solitude, the dread of sleep
> beside a comrade whose soul had lost God's light.

41 /74 **The Wish** 1840

Oil on canvas 35½x 27⁷/₈ins (90x71cm)
Signed on verso 'T. Von. Holst Pinx./1840' with
sketches of a face and several hands (canvas now lined)
Prov: Lord Northwick, Thirlestane House Collection
sold Phillips, 26/7/1859 (1161) £110-5s, to Joseph
Lovegrove FSA, Elton House, Gloucester, then Christies
Sale, 31/3/1883
Exh: London, British Institution, 1841 (255)
London, Brian Sewell

An appraisal of this important picture, by the present compiler,
was published in the *Burlington Magazine* in February 1978.
It provided the first direct evidence of the link of influence
proclaimed by Dante Gabriel Rossetti, of Holst as "one of the
few connecting links between the earlier and sound period of
English colour and method in painting, and that revival of which
so many signs have in late years been apparent"; in essence a
bridge of influence from earlier English painters, such as Fuseli
and Blake, to that of the Pre-Raphaelites.

Rossetti provides the link himself by recalling that 'Specimens
from his hand existed in the late Northwick Collection, now

dispersed', which is where he must have seen *The Wish* which he used as the pictorial source for his first widely published poem, *The Card Dealer: or, Vingt-Et-Un. From A Picture* (*Atheaneum* 23 October 1852, reproduced in the 1994 catalogue, p.103). The poem was written in 1848.

The strong *penchant* of Rossetti for drawing subjects of the supernatural and fantastic are well documented, but Holst's tendency to paint such disturbing subjects onto canvas for exhibition is the universally quoted reason for his scant recognition by the public. However the success of *The Wish*, and other centrally placed female subjects, demonstrates that Holst's new found confidence and firmness of form in the 1840s managed to provide him, at last, with a successful pictorial formula that was much appreciated by connoisseurs and some of the leading aristocratic collectors of the day.

The attractive, oval-faced prototype for the female subject is found in several sketches by Holst and may well be based on the artist's fiancé, the twenty years-old Amelia Thomasina Symmes-Villard, whom he married the following year. A striking chiaroscuro induces a disturbing, almost menacing quality to the characteristically placed central figure, enhanced by the lurid red glow emanating from behind her and the strong light source, from her left, which serves to accentuate both her bosom and the action of her hands against the contrasting darkness of the rest of the scene. The paint has been confidently applied, layer by layer over a dark base, to produce the rich blend of colour and sparkling depth in small details that were features admired by the Pre-Raphaelites and, as William Rossetti later explained, the reason why they gathered to dine at Campbell's Scotch Stores restaurant, Beak Street, 'as it was hung around with pictures by Theodore Von Holst.'

Fig.26 D.G. Rossetti, *The Card Player* [Surtees 234]

This picture became a seminal source for the PRB. As well as inspiring Rossetti's poem, it also led to his large pencil drawing of *The Card Player* (fig 26) and to Millais's famous small panel of *The Bridesmaid*, of 1851, now in the Fitzwilliam Museum, along with its companion *Emily Patmore* of the same date. The

latter's compositional source is slightly less sure since Coventry Patmore unfortunately cut off the bottom third of the picture after complaining it portrayed a too severe likeness of his late wife.

An observation of relevance to the present exhibition is the mystic romanticism displayed here by Theodor which is also evident later in the work of his great-nephew Gustav Holst. *The Wish* and *The Planets Suite* both come from the same passionate mystic stable whose origin seems to emanate back through epochs of Nordic mist.

The von Holst family association with Cheltenham would have made them aware of Theodor's important painting there but whether this filtered through to Gustav is not known. Before Gustav's birth *The Wish* had been sold in the forced dispersal of the Northwick Collection in 1859. But it moved only a few miles away to Gloucester, where it remained for the next quarter of a century.

A possible literary source for Holst may be Frederic Schoberl's (1775-1853) poem *The Wish*, published in the *Forget Me Not* annual of 1829:

> 'Tis sweet along the pebbled shore
> The solitary path to trace,
> To list the billows' endless roar,
> To witness their eternal chase.
>
> 'Tis sweet – how sweet! – at dewey eve,
> 'Neath jessamine and woodbine bow'rs,
> Where Fancy loves fair scenes to weave,
> To muse away the moonlight hours.
>
> But sweeter far to gaze, I ween,
> On Woman's soul-illumin'd eye,
> When heav'nly thoughts light up her mien
> With more than earthly ecstasy:
>
> To watch the gems of pity start,
> And on that eye's soft fringes hang –
> Mute language of the tender heart,
> Pure as the fount from which they sprang:
>
> To drink with greedy ear the stream
> Of music from her witching voice,
> That melts the soul to sorrow's theme,
> Or bids its ev'ry nerve rejoice:
>
> To find in pain, in weal, [in] woe,
> A pillow on the one-loved breast –
> Let me, ye Fates such transport know!
> Take wealth, and fame, and all the rest!

Schoberl was Henry Colburn's founding partner of the New Monthly Magazine in 1814 and his son, William, became Coburn's assistant. With these connections it seems reasonable to suppose that Holst was familiar with the family as well as Schoberl's literary output.

42 /75   **The Bride** 1842
(Shelley, *Ginevra*, 9-12)

Oil on Windsor and Newton canvas, 35½x27½ins
(90x70cm)
Signed on verso 'T Von Holst/1842' with an outline
sketch of two male figures
Prov: Duchess of Sutherland, Stafford Collection; Miss
Susannah Newbould, Bolebrook Castle, sold Christie's,
10th October 1969, lot 93, to Gray for 290 gns.
England, Private Collection

This is Holst's most popular picture and the finest of three
versions known to exist. The present 'Stafford version' was
purchased by the Duchess of Sutherland from the British
Institution Exhibition in 1842. It was so admired by the third
Marquess of Lansdowne that he persuaded Holst to paint a larger
version (fig.15) that was hung *solus* in the breakfast-room of his
magnificent house in Berkeley Square. Significantly Millais was
a regular guest of Lord Lansdowne and would have been aware
of the painting which probably inspired his design commissioned
to illustrate a book of songs (fig.29) in 1868. In addition his own

small panel of *The Bride* painted ten years before this displays a notable similarity of subject and simple composition.

The fine finish, bright fresco-like gilding and literary theme of Holst's picture also appealed to other members of the Pre-Raphaelite circle. In his *Supplementary* to Gilchrist's posthumous *Life of William Blake*, published in 1863, Dante Gabriel Rossetti recollected a few years earlier seeing the present version: 'A most beautiful work by him - a female head or half figure-among the pictures at Stafford House.' At about the same time as contributing this appraisal of Holst for Gilchrist, Rossett painted his small but equally exquisite *Girl at a Lattice* (1994 Cat..fig.29), which can be seen as a blend of *The Bride* and influences such as Etty's wistful *Portrait of a Girl* (fig.27), which possibly depicts his grand-daughter and housekeeper, Bessy. Rossetti was not alone among the PRB in admiring Etty, as well as Holst, and Gilchrist's previous biography had been on the life of the older artist. Additionally a watercolour sketch of *The Bride* (cat.55), with acknowledgement to Holst, appears in a commonplace book of Rossetti's friend the sculptor Alexander Munro.

Another artist's watercolour version of *The Bride* has been notified to me recently by Alison Smith. It is by George Howard (Castle Howard Cat. PWC0207), 9th Earl of Carlisle, who was a friend and patron of Burne-Jones. In a personal observation Franny Moyle has proposed that the present picture may have influenced Burne-Jones in his romanticised neo-Renaissance portrait study, *Vespertina Quies*, painted in 1893 and now at Tate Britain.

Many years ago Brian Sewell pointed out the influence of Italian Renaissance portraiture on Holst's work along with the later derivations by Dutch realists and German romantics. In terms of composition *The Bride* does provide a link from the romanticized neo-renaissance ideals of the German Nazarene school to that of the Pre-Raphaelites. In 1810 Friedrich Overbeck had painted a seminal casement portrait of his fellow Nazarene Franz Pforr (fig.28). He was centrally placed in an arched casement against a medieval Italian setting. It is a bold and simple representation of the romantic Teutonic artist 'finding himself' and flourishing in the lush warmth of the southern climate and culture. Bold and simple romantic compositions of this type found a natural resonance in Holst who responded with variations of his own although these were not of the serene and devotional order of the Nazarenes.

Gert Schiff, in his pioneering *Burlington Magazine* article on Holst, noted that the artist found Shelley's poem *Ginevra* compelling enough to illustrate it at several times in his career. It is a tragic story of a young Florentine girl who is reluctantly to be married to an aged nobleman. After the wedding ceremony she takes leave of her young lover for the last time and finally, as the guests assemble at the banquet, her husband finds her dead on her bridal bed. The illustrated lines occur earlier:

> Ginevra from the nuptial altar went,
> The vows to which her lips had sworn assent
> Rung in her brain still with a jarring din,
> Deafening the lost intelligence within.

Fig.27 William Etty *Portrait of a Girl* (unlocated)

Fig.28 Friederick Overbeck *Portrait of Franz Pforr* 1810

Fig.29 J.E. Millais *A Reverie* 1868 (unlocated)

43 /76   **Portrait of a Lady with Spanish Headdress**
c.1840-43

Oil on canvas, 30x24¹/₈ins (76.1x63cm)
Inscr. 'Matilda, wife of Stoker Esq/Dublin' on old label,
rear of stretcher
England, Private Collection

The attribution is based on stylistic grounds and does not accord
to the description of the *Spanish Lady*, Holst's last exhibit at the
Royal Academy in 1843, which is given in the 1897 Lansdowne
Collection catalogue. The composition is reminiscent of both
Leonardo's *Mona Lisa* and neo-Renaissance Biedermeier
paintings by the Nazarene painter Friedrich Wilhelm von
Schadow (1788-1862), and Joseph Karl Stieler's (1781-1858)
series of 'Beauties' for Ludwig I, which Holst may have been
familiar with from his occasional trips to Germany. Intriguingly
it also bears a compositional
and tonal resemblance to a
painting by the Irish painter
Richard Rothwell, *Portrait
of a Young Man* (fig.30).
Both artists knew each
other and had been students
of Sir Thomas Lawrence.
For Holst's vitriolic reply
to Rothwell, regarding an
unwelcome missive to his
father, see cat.7.

Fig.30 Richard Rothwell, *Portrait of a
Young Man* (unlocated)

BOOKS AND PRINTS

44   Mary Shelley, *Frankenstein*, Colburn and Bentley,
/39,40   *Standard Novels*, 1831

Frankenstein and His Monster
Frontispiece steel engraving by W. Chevalier, 9.3x7.1cm

Frankenstein, having learned the secret of imparting life into
inanimate remains, has just observed the first stirrings of the
creature of his creation. The lines illustrated are: 'By the
glimmer of the half-extinguished light, I saw the dull yellow eye
of the creature open; it breathed hard and a convulsive motion
agitated its limbs, . . . I rushed out of the room.'

Mary Shelley's "late gothic" novel was first published
anonymously in London in 1818. From then until now it has
been regarded as sensationally imaginative, prophetic and
extraordinarily popular, becoming an icon of "horror" - a
man-made man - that has fascinated every age in between and
inspired countless derivatives. Holst was the first published
illustrator and his two designs accompanied the 1831 edition
where Mary Shelley was identified as the author for the
first time. By association with its famous subject, Holst's
frontispiece design has appeared in almost every illustrated
survey of the *Frankenstein* cult to have been published.

45
/41,42   Frederick Schiller, *The Ghost-Seer*, Colburn and
Bentley, *Standard Novels*, 1831
London, Max Browne

Appearance of the Greek Lady
Frontispiece steel engraving by W. Chevalier 9.8x7.2cm

The Praying Man
Title-page steel engraved vignette by W. Chevalier
8.2x5.3cm

46 /45   Anna Jameson, *The Beauties of the Court of King
Charles II*. Published for H. Colburn by R. Bentley,
Oct. 1832
London, Max Browne

Frontispiece Decoration (2 details shown)
Lithograph by Charles Wagstaff, 9³/₈x 6¾ins
(23.6x17.1cm)

The elaborately decorated border is strongly influenced by the
popular German style of page decoration of the period. Anna
Jameson was an influential advocate of this and commended
Holst's contribution in this respect although the two small
Faustian designs featured in the border decoration are somewhat
incongruous with respect to the main body of plates engraved by
the author's father.

47 /46   Edward Lytton Bulwer, *The Pilgrims of the Rhine*,
Saunders and Otley, 1834.
London, Max Browne

The Fallen Star
Steel engraved vignette by R. Staines, 3 1/2x3 1/8ins
(9x7.8cm) facing p.175.

This shows the influence of the vast and apocalyptic designs of
the highly popular painter and illustrator John Martin. Holst and
Martin were fellow exhibitors and illustrators on many occasions
and Bulwer was a patron and admirer of both artists. Martin's
masterly series of mezzotint illustrations to Milton's *Paradise
Lost* had been published in 1825 just before his large plate
of *Belshazzar's Feast*, from which Holst has adopted several
elements such as the shining apparition on the left, starlight sky,
lightning flashes and conical mountain derived from the Tower
of Babel.

48 /62 S.C. Halls (Ed.) *Book of Gems*, 1837
London, Max Browne

A bearded Man in Renaissance costume looks in terror at a Sundial

Steel engraved vignette by W.H. Simmons, 3¼x2¾ins (8.1x7.1cm), on p.43, entitled *Too Late* to illustrate a passage from Young's *Night Thoughts.*

The similarity of this figure to the artist's self-portrayal of himself as *Macbeth in the Witches Cavern* (cat.37) is marked as it is also to that in *Speranza* (fig.31) a design by Kenny Meadows, another artist associated with Samuel Carter Hall's circle. As well as featuring in his own works Holst would not have been averse to appearing in those by others. If this is the case he co-stars with a muse of obvious charms and both appear as if in the Byronic set-piece of ' Manfred and the Witch of the Alps' although this is not the given subject.

Fig.31 K. Meadows, *Speranza* engraving

49 Edward Bulwer Lytton, *Alice; or, The Mysteries*
Harper & Brothers, 82   Cliff St., New-York, 1842
London, Max Browne

Caesarini and the Soldier in the Forest

Steel engraving by A. Dick, 10x7.2 cm, after Holst's painting, facing title page.

'The fire blazed red at last. On a little mound -
shaded by a semicircle of huge trees - sat the
Outlaws of Human Reason'

This adds another piece to the puzzle concerning Holst's American connections that include a projected trip to New York (see 1994 cat.31) and the emigration of the engraver John Sartain (see cat.51). The engraver of the present plate, Alexander Dick, was Scottish but had established himself in New York by 1833. Lytton's novel was published in London in 1838 and so Holst's painting was presumably engraved some time after this at Dick's workshop before the New York edition of 1842 or, possibly, by another engraver commissioned by Dick who may have accomplished this elsewhere.

I am grateful to David Weinglass for not only informing me of this American edition with Holst's illustration, but, with characteristic generosity, presenting it as a gift. A double benefit was the consequent identification of the subject of the painting (cat.40) that had also recently come to light.

50 /71   **The Raising of Jairus' Daughter** (1845)
(*St.Luke*, 8, 41)

Steel engraving by G. Periam, 10 1/8x6 1/8ins
(25.8x15.5cm)
After Holst's large British Institution prize-winning
picture of 1841 (1), now lost.
Published by S.C. Hall, with a critique, in *Gems of
European Art*, 1845, p.53 f.; Virtue's *Bible* nd, Ed.
Mathew Henry, Part II, St. Luke, opp p.442
Lit: Gilchrist (Rossetti's *Supplementary*) 1863, p.380;
Bell Scott 1892, p.163
London, Max Browne

This unusual effort by Holst, originally painted the year of
his marriage, can be seen, perhaps, as an attempt to balance
his reputation for extravagant romance in order to secure a
firmer financial base for the future, this is also indicated by his
increased portraiture exhibited this year.

However, although highly praised at the time by critics such
as Samuel Carter Hall, the editing-publisher of the *Art-Union*
journal, the original life-sized picture had still not found a
purchaser over two years after the artist's death. It won the 50
guinea prize at the British Institution in 1841 and Holst was
praised for having at last produced a work that:

> . . is, in all respects, admirable; it is a grand composition;
> a great effort in the school about which we talk so much,
> and for which we do so little. The figure of the Redeemer
> is happily portrayed, and the whole group is arranged with
> consummate skill and delicacy; there is no straining after
> dramatic effect; the touching incident has been illustrated
> with the purest truth . . . Music was kept, while painting was
> rejected by "the Fathers of the Reformation." Thus was not
> only lost a powerful auxiliary to religion, but the main prop
> of National Art was taken away. Thenceforward, Art had no
> high aim; its efforts became nearly, if not altogether, directed
> to perpetuations of comparative trifles. And now, as in the
> case before us , when an artist seeks to restore it to its most
> valuable and most legitimate purpose, he must pay the penalty
> of being "in advance of his age;" and keep the picture, as to
> him, so much useless lumber--to occupy a large portion of
> the small room in which he works. Consigning to oblivion
> that which might afford enjoyment and instruction to tens of
> thousands, if placed where its silent but impressive lessons
> could be taught. We are, however, it is to be hoped on the eve
> of a more auspicious day - a day that shall witness the revival
> of the Arts in Great Britain.

We may smile at the pious Victorian tone of this appraisal but it
is from the pen of one of the most influential critics of the day
and reflects the taste of a wide audience. It is also, of course, a
rallying cry for English Art, answered by the formation of the
Pre-Raphaelite Brotherhood three years later.

Ironically the painting was not seen in such glowing terms by all
contemporaries and admirers, for in Rossetti's opinion:

> A notable instance of his comparative weakness in subjects
> of pure dignity, may be found in what has been pronounced
> his best work, and was probably the most "successful" at the
> time of its production; that is, the *Raising of Jairus' Daughter*,
> which was lately in the gallery at the Pantheon in Oxford
> Street, and probably still remains there.

In fact Rossetti had pinned his colours to the mast many years
earlier by using Holst's more pagan picture also shown at the
British Institution in 1841, *The Wish* (cat.41), as the pictorial
source for his first published poem, *The Card Dealer*. *The
Art-Union* was less enthusiastic about this as it was 'a little too
much, perhaps, in his former style, and therefore less pleasing.
Its execution is, however, absolutely faultless.'

The Biblical story of Jairus' Daughter is related in several
gospels; those of St. Matthew, St. Mark and St. Luke. The latter
provides an appropriate text for the present work where Jairus, a
synagogue ruler, begs Jesus to come to heal his dying daughter.
He agrees but on the way they are told that she has meanwhile

died. The lines illustrated are:

> And when he came into the house, he suffered no man to go in, save Peter, and James, and John, and the father and the mother of the maiden.
> And all wept, and bewailed her: but he said, Weep not; she is not dead, but sleepeth.
> And they laughed him to scorn, knowing that she was dead.
> And he put them all out, and took her by the hand, and called, saying, Maid, arise.
> And her spirit came again, and she arose straightaway: and he commanded to give her meat.

51 /72 **The Raising of Jairus' Daughter** (1846)
(*St.Luke*, 8, 41)

Mezzotint engraving by John Sartain, 12.3.x9.3cm, after Holst's large, now lost, British Institution prize-winning picture of 1841 (1) or the plate by Periam above (cat.50) Plate Inscr. 'Painted by Theodore Von Holst | Engraved by J. Sartain | *Raising of Jairus' Daughter*.'
Published with accompanying poem, by Robert Hamilton, in *The Mayflower*, Boston, 1846, p.105
London, Max Browne

This small mezzotint is by the artist's engraver acquaintance, John Sartain (1808-1897), who was to have engraved a planned series of *Faust* illustrations by Holst many years earlier. Sartain emigrated to Philadelphia in 1830, where he established himself successfully, during a period of great cultural change and economic hardship for artists in England.

It can be clearly seen that some license has been taken in this engraving, compared to the definitive larger reproduction of the previous year (cat.50). Most notably the Saviour has lost his halo, one of his apostles has lost his moustache and the vase on the table has changed shape. It is one of the few examples of engravings after Holst to be published in the U.S.A.

WORKS BY OTHER ARTISTS

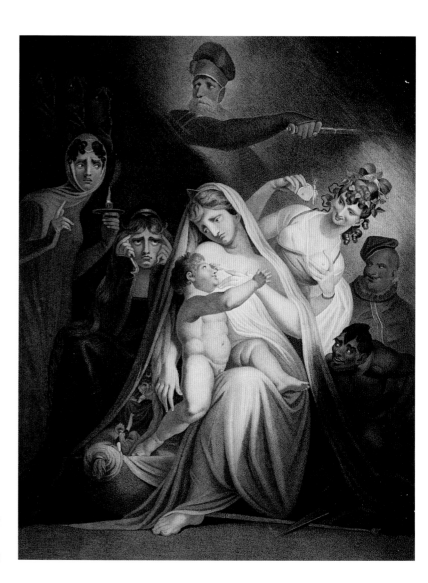

Henry Fuseli (1741-1825)

52 **The Nursery of Shakespeare (**1805-1810)

Stipple engraving 51.8x40.5 cm by Moses Haughton after Fuseli's painting
Lit. Schiff 1973 (S.1202a); Weinglass 1994 (288.I)
London, Max Browne

Henry Fuseli, Keeper of the Royal Academy, was Holst's first and foremost art teacher and influence. This eccentric, inspiring and vivacious master died when his pupil was only fifteen years old but nevertheless left such an indelible mark that reliable attributions of many of their works proved insurmountable until Gert Schiff's monumental scholarship finally untangled them in the 1960s.

From childhood Holst had been steeped in the intensely dramatic world of Fuseli. It was a powerful 18th century synthesis of the heroes, villains and magic of western literature and life that had challenged Fuseli's pictorial expression into creating a unique blend of historical and supernatural imagery. Holst was alone in lapping this up and becoming a bridge to the later masters of the Pre-Raphaelite Brotherhood.

Moses Haughton (1773-1849) was Fuseli's personal engraver-in-residence and spent most of his time working on plates of Fuseli's Milton Gallery paintings, an epic exhibition project that had failed commercially. This is the only Haughton engraving of a Fuseli subject derived from Shakespeare and provides a tours-de-force of Fuseli's idiosyncratic response to his literary idol. It is also an excellent example of the wellspring of motifs that Holst's master provided that was much exploited by his pupil.

Dante Gabriel Rossetti (1828-82)

53 The Raven 1846
(Poe's poem *The Raven*, 1845)

Pen and brown ink, 13³/₈x9½ins
Signed with monogram and dated 'June/46'
Lit. Surtees 1971 (19), Marsh 1999, p.29
Prov: Alexander Munro and by family descent
London, Katharine Macdonald

Having been reproduced many times, this drawing is a well known, characteristic and classic example of why Rossetti can be regarded as the next generation successor to the 'satanic school' after that of Fuseli and Holst. Like his predecessors, Rossetti's *penchant* for the supernatural, demonic and erotic lay alongside his more conventional English 19th century upbringing, influences and interests and demonstrate why he has become its most fascinating and written about figure. No one else has such a rich blend of cultural and personal extremes that can be related to by such a wide audience. He was both christian and pagan, refined and primitive and the aptly titled PRB study, *Desperate Romantics* by Franny Moyle, is the most recent to show this.

Although the execution and tonality of this drawing are closer to contemporary magazine illustrations, an iconographic analysis shows a line of influence to Holst that reaches back to Blake and Fuseli, particularly in the background and fairy figures. All the elements of the design can be found in Holst's painting of *A Dream after Reading Goethe's Walspurgisnacht* (1994 frontispiece), where the male figure remains sitting, seemingly unmoved, but amidst a similar throng of lilliputian and life-sized apparitions. Rossetti's distressed figure however appears overwhelmed by the frenzied claustrobia of his spectral visions. This could be seen as a graphic prophecy of Rossetti's own mental state, in years to come, as he found himself in the middle of situations of half-finished work, enticing females, threatening figures and death set against a background of cultural history and refinement.

The stanza illustrated is:

'Be that word our sign of parting, bird or fiend!' I shrieked upstarting -
'Get thee back into the tempest and the Night's Plutonian shore!
Leave no black plume as a token of that lie thy soul hath spoken!
Leave my loneliness unbroken! - quit the bust above my door!
Take thy beak from out my heart, and take thy form from off my door!'
Quoth the raven, 'Nevermore'.

Dante Gabriel Rossetti

54   La Belle Dame Sans Merci 1848
(Keats's poem *La Belle Dame Sans Merci*, 1820)

Pen, pencil and sepia 11x5¾ins (16.3x19.9cm)
Signed with monogram and dated 'April/48'
Lit. Surtees 1971 (32), Marsh 1999, p.41
Prov: Alexander Munro and by family descent
London, Katharine Macdonald

This important and attractive drawing by Rossetti is strangely
not illustrated in the Surtees catalogue-raisonné and is therefore
little known. It was drawn for the Cyclographic Society and
is the earliest one to survive with a 'criticism sheet' which is

dated March 1848. It was well received by the members but
drew technical criticism for the: "Mouth of the lady too small"
(Green), "man's left leg badly drawn . . but conception excellent
and worth painting" (Millais) and "beautifully designed, good
subject . . . would paint well" (Holman Hunt). Most importantly
it was Rossetti's first formal portrayal of a *femme fatale*, and
therefore represents an early personification of his image of a
desirable lover, at the time he was first meeting other members
of the nascent PRB.

The 'Belle Dame' is delicately drawn and emanates a cute-
factor that classes her as an early Rossetti 'stunner'. She bears
more than a passing resemblance to Holst's 'Zurich *Bertalda*'
(1994 cat.61) in stance although not playing a victim here. She
also anticipates the (slightly sweeter) later medieval heroines
of Arthur 'Cherry' Hughes (see Hughes's sketch of this subject
52.2 and others, including *April Love*, in Roberts, 1997) and
both artists would have picked up hints from Holst in this regard.
Interestingly one of the Cyclographic group, Richard Burchett,
commented on Rossetti's dog that does not appear in Keats's
poem but is nevertheless useful in conveying its instinctive dread
of a supernatural presence. In Holst's 'Cheltenham *Bertalda*'
painting (cat.36) a black cat with glowing eyes can be seen in
exactly the same location. Rossetti would have been familiar
with such characteristic devices by Holst which, possibly,
inspired his doeful hound.

Pre-Raphaelite circle

55   The Bride [c.1845-55]

Pen, pencil and watercolour
Inscribed 'T Von Holst' mounted on page 167 in a
commonplace book of Alexander Munro with inscribed
stanza from a poem by Goethe (translation by Edgar A.
Bowring, 1853) on facing page.
Prov: Alexander Munro thence by family descent
London, Katharine Macdonald

As a talented young stone-mason Alexander Munro (1825-71)
had been taken under the wing of the Duchess of Sutherland.
She was a fervent patron of the arts and in 1844 introduced him
to his first employer in London, Charles Barry, designer of the
new Houses of Parliament. Two years earlier she had snapped up
Holst's painting of *The Bride* (cat.42) at the British Institution
exhibition. If Munro is the author it is reasonable to suppose
that the present sketch is one that he made from memory
sometime later and perhaps after enthusing with Rossetti about
the earlier artist that they both admired. Rossetti was only
twelve years old when the painting was exhibited in 1842 but he
later recalled seeing it at Stafford House and it may have been
a prompt from Munro that lead him in that direction. Munro's
notebooks are known to contain sketches by other artists such as
Rossetti, Millais and Hughes and we look forward to positively
identifying the author of this one .

Note on the Illustrations

I would like to express my thanks to the many enthusiastic and hospitable owners for allowing me access to examine and photograph their paintings and drawings and for permission to reproduce them here. In some cases I must apologise to owners of works in my files that have been illustrated as scholarly reference but I have not been able to identify or contact. I would be very pleased to hear from them and provide a copy of the catalogue on request.

A comparison with the painting (of which three versions are known) immediately shows how free the copying has been. The direction of the sitter has been reversed, the supporting arm raised, the other arm now lies along a balustrade and the bas-relief cupid has been retained on the left side.

The small watercolour has been mounted onto a right-hand page in one of Munro's commonplace books opposite an inscription of a translated passage from a ballad by Goethe. This translation by Edgar Bowring was first published in 1853 and the stanza inscribed is:

> I'm rich indeed to me is given
> That godlike prize, that gift of heaven,
> To be content when these are mine:
> A maiden with her kisses ready,
> A conscience pure, friendly, true and steady
> And every day a flask of wine.

Appendix I

ITEMS BY THEODOR VON HOLST IN CHELTENHAM MUSEUMS

When the Holst Birthplace Museum became independent in 2000 ownership of works included in Imogen Holst's original endowment and works purchased since then have remained with Cheltenham Art Gallery & Museum. As a consequence the works on loan sometimes varies.

PAINTINGS

All the paintings by Holst located at either museum are included as entries in the Catalogue section. After the exhibition it is hoped that *Macbeth, Banquo and the Witches* (Cat.37, Private Collection) will remain at the Holst Birthplace Museum on long term loan.

CHELTENHAM ART GALLERY & MUSEUM

DRAWINGS

Seated Woman Wearing a Long Dress, pencil 22.1x14cm, signed (1978.179).*

Naason (after Michelangelo's lunette in the Sistine Chapel), pencil 18x21.6cm, inscr. 'The Student', signed (1978.177).*

Studies of Limbs, pencil, pen and brown ink, 16.5x25.6cm, signed (1978.180).*

Young Woman Seated with a Man with Moustache and Imperial, pen and brown ink 27.9x25.2cm (1978.178).*

Faust in his Study, pencil 16.6x16.6cm (1982.1213).

Mephistopheles and the Student in Faust's Study, pencil 21.6x18.5cm. [Cat.12]

Decorative Design for Ironwork, pencil 32.2x20cm (1982.1214).

Bearded Man and other Figures, pencil 24.8x32.4cm (1980.2012).

Distraught Man with Hands Clasped to his Head, pencil 21x19.7cm (1975.82.1). [Cat.31]

Mother Teaching a Child and other Figures, pencil 29.5x25cm (1980.2012)

Man holding a Mask and Dagger, pencil 15.7x14.8 (1975.82.2)

Study of Woman in Classical Robe, pencil 20x9.1cm (1980.2013)

Sketch of a Tree Trunk, pencil 19.1x15.3cm (1977.322). [Cat.33]

* purchased from Colnaghi and donated by Imogen Holst in 1974.

HOLST BIRTHPLACE MUSEUM

DRAWINGS

Portrait of a Young Woman, brown and red chalk, 8½x6¼ins (1969.172). [Ownership of this drawing has descended through the Holst family but its attribution is questionable]

Distraught Young Woman with Her Head in her Hand, black chalk 5¼x4¼ins (1974.5). [Cat. 32]

LETTERS

Theodor, Gustavus and Constantia to their Parents (with watercolour self-portrait), 24 April 1827 (1984.1). [Cat.1]

Theodor, Gustavus and Constantia to their Parents (with watercolour portrait of Constantia), 21 May 1827 (1984.2/3). [see fig.5]

Theodor to Richard Rothwell, 21 August 1830. [Cat.7]

Theodor to Parents and Sisters, 7 October 1832 (1981.1472 - possibly a first draft of the letter, below, sent a week later).

Theodor and Gustavus to Parents and Sisters, 13 October 1832 (1981.1473) [Cat.2]

Theodor to William Chamberlain, 31 October 1840. [Cat.8]

Theodor to Parents and Sisters, 7 October 1832 (detail)

APPENDIX II

THE MUNRO-HOLST SKETCHBOOK
(cat.34)

The sketch-book is without covers, is in two parts on laid paper watermarked 'CT' / '1796' (22.5 x 17 cm) and has some pages torn out. It comprises 57 well-thumbed double-sided pages featuring a variety of sketches, notes and letter drafts from the last half of Holst's career. The first date recorded is 1834 and the last is implicit in the draft of a letter to Lord Lytton, of 1843, concerning the artist's offer to paint a grand romantic portrait of the celebrated author and politician (which still hangs above the main staircase at Knebworth House).

It is the first sketchbook by Holst to come to light and has been passed down through the family descendants of the sculptor Alexander Munro (1825-1871)*. How Munro acquired it is unknown but there is a strong possibility that it was through another Scottish sculptor, Patric Park (1811-55), who was a close friend of Holst and later Munro.

The sketchbook received its public unveiling at Tate Britain's *Gothic Nightmares* exhibition in 2006 (Tate cat.73). It was shown open at pages 6v/7 which features *A Skeletal Bride* (see opp.) and sketches of male caricatures in medieval costume.

Particularly intriguing are pages containing a list of proposed or realised subjects, *Night Sketches*, along with several significant names of individuals associated with the artist, and a title-page design for a projected *Faust Fancies by TvH*.

The significance of the names appearing alongside *Night Sketches* are as follows:

'Mrs. Wainewright' – the wife of the extraordinary Thomas Griffiths Wainewright, Holst's friend, who saw her husband for the last time, before his conviction and transportation to Tasmania, in 1837 and emigrated with their son to the USA, in 1851, after the trust embezzled by her husband was repaid by the Bank of England.

'Mrs. Jameson' – the indefatigable writer on the visual arts, and champion of the German School, during the 1830/40s.

'Mr. Thomas' – the lawyer, collector and dealer who was associated with artists including John Martin and Millais and (always with an eye for a bargain) accumulated the finest collection of works by Holst after his death.

In view of the limited space available here, it seems best to reproduce a representative selection of pages rather than a log of the total contents. The illustrations are numbered according to their page numbers in the sketchbook.

* I would like to express my grateful thanks to Katharine Macdonald, grand-daughter of the sculptor and guardian of his collection, for her always generous advice, hospitality and support, and for the extended loan of the sketchbook many years ago.

SELECTED PAGES

3. *A Cloaked Woman Kneeling in Prayer*, pencil and pen

12. *A Man Sawing*, pencil and pen

6v/6. *A Skeletal Bride / A Skeletal Monk* (face traced through), pencil / pencil and pen

9v. *A Man Playing the Devil at a Table*, pencil and pen

15. *Portrait Head of Faust with Mephistopheles and Margaret*, pencil and black chalk

16v/17. *Huldbrand on Horseback is startled by Kuhleborn/ A Couple in Medieval Costume*, black chalk

15v/16 *Seated Couple Embracing watched by a fallen angel* (perhaps Paolo and Francesca) red and black chalk / *Stamding couple embracing in Medieval Costume*, black chalk

33. *'Faust Fancies' title-page design*, pencil (inscr. 'Faust Fancies by TvH' / 'Dragon smoking a pipe' / (indec)

18. *A Standing Warrior* (copied from Delacroix), red and black chalk

21v. *Group of Men seen from behind*, black chalk (inscr. '(?) witnessing an execution'

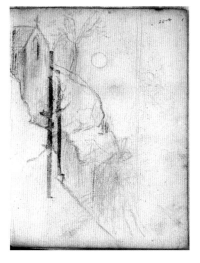

25 *Chapel overlooking a Mountainous Landscape*, pencil and black chalk

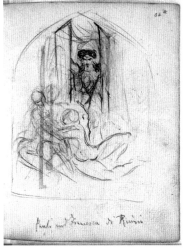

34. *Paolo and Francesca di Rimini*, pencil and black chalk

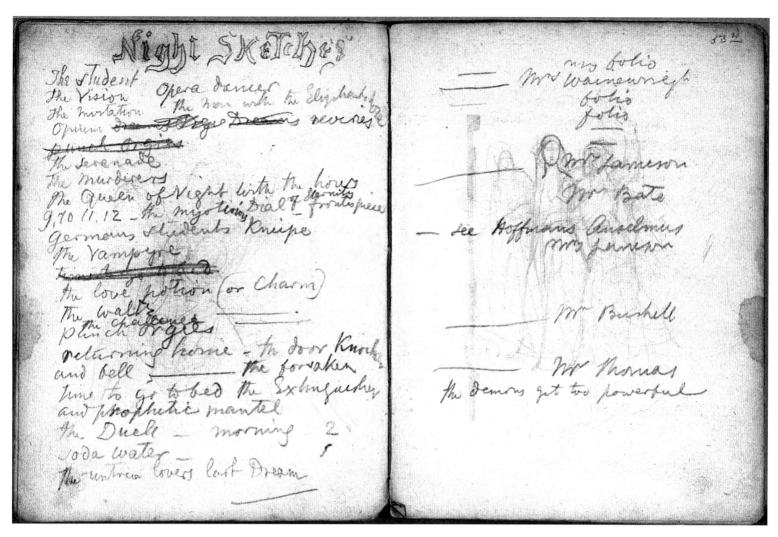

52v/ 53, *Night Sketches* – a list of 'dark' picture subjects / listing of associated names, pencil

54, *Portrait sketch of a Young Woman*, pencil

57 *Young Woman kneeling before a Window*, pencil

SELECT BIBLIOGRAPHY

(These titles principally update the 1994 bibliography and are published in London unless otherwise stated)

BOOKS

Browne, M., *The Romantic Art of Theodor Von Holst (1810-44)*, 1994.

Funnel, P. & Warner, M., *Millais: Portraits* (National Portrait Gallery exhibition catalogue), 1999.

Griffiths, A. & Carey, F., *German Printmaking in the Age of Goethe*, 1994.

Kinnear, L. & Fletcher, C., *The Lediards and Whatleys of Gloucestershire: A Holst Family History*, Cheltenham, 2009.

Macdonald, K., *Alexander Munro: Pre-Raphaelite Associate* in *Pre-Raphaelite Sculpture Nature and Imagination in British Sculpture 1848-1914* (Eds. Read, B. & Barnes, J.), 1991.

Marsh, J., *Dante Gabriel Rossetti: Painter and Poet*, 1999.

McCalman, I. (Ed.), *An Oxford Companion to the Romantic Age British Culture 1776-1832*, Oxford, 1999.

Mitchel, L., *Bulwer Lytton: The Rise and Fall of a Victorian Man of Letters*, 2003

Motion, A., *Wainewright The Poisoner*, 2000.

Moyle, F., *Desperate Romantics The Private Lives of the Pre-Raphaelites*, 2009.

Myrone, M., *Henry Fuseli*, 2001

Myrone, M., GOTHIC NIGHTMARES *Fuseli, Blake and the Romantic Imagination* (Tate Britain exhibition catalogue), 2006.

Oxford Dictionary of National Biography, 2004 (online website at www.oxforddnb.com).

Ponder, S, *Wightwick Manor*, National Trust, 1993 (Forward by Anthea Mander Lahr).

Prettejohn, E. (Ed.), *After the Pre-Raphaelites*, Manchester, 1999.

Roberts, L., ARTHUR HUGHES *His Life and Works* (catalogue raisonné), Woodbridge, 1997.

Rosenfeld, J. & Smith, A., *Millais* (Tate Britain exhibition catalogue), 2007.

Royal Academy, *Victorian Fairy Painting* (exhibition catalogue), 1998.

Salvadori, F. (Ed.), JOHN FLAXMAN *The illustrations for Dante's Divine Comedy*, 2004

Treuherz, J., Prettejohn, E. & Becker, E., *Dante Gabriel Rossetti* (Walker exhibition catalogue), Liverpool, 2003.

Weinglass, D., *Füssli pittore di Shakespeare Pittura e teatro 1775-1825* (Fondazione Magnani Rocca exhibition catalogue), Parma, 1997.

Wood, C., *Fairies in Victorian Art*, Woodbridge, 2000.

Young, G (Ed.), *Early Victorian England 1830-1865*, (2 vols.) Oxford, 1934.

PERIODICALS

Allen, B., *Apollo*, July 1994, pp.53-54 (review).

Browne, M., *Blake an Illustrated Quarterly*, Rochester, Winter 1995/6, pp.78-81.

Butlin, M., *Burlington Magazine*, July 1994, p.476 (review).

Ionides, J., *Pre-Raphaelite Society Review*, Birmingham, Autumn 1994, pp.8-9 (review)

Sewell, B., *London Evening Standard*, 5 May 1994, p.43 (review).

Theodor von Holst website - www.vonholst.info

Additionally numerous websites searched and selected via *Google* and, particularly useful, *Google Images*.